Philosophy as a Literary Art

Despite philosophers' growing interest in the relation between philosophy and literature in general, over the last few decades comparatively few studies have been published dealing more narrowly with the literary aspects of philosophical texts. The relationship between philosophy and literature is too often taken to be "literature as philosophy" and very rarely "philosophy as literature." It is the dissatisfaction with this one-sidedness that lies at the heart of the present volume. Philosophy has nothing to lose by engaging in a serious process of literary self-analysis. On the contrary, such an exercise would most likely make it stronger, more sophisticated, more playful and especially more self-reflexive. By not moving in this direction, philosophy places itself in the position of not following what has been deemed, since Socrates at least, the worthiest of all philosophical ideals: self-knowledge.

This book was originally published as a special issue of *The European Legacy*.

Costica Bradatan is Associate Professor of Honors at Texas Tech University, USA. He is the author or editor (co-editor) of several books, including *Philosophy, Society and The Cunning of History in Eastern Europe* (2012) and most recently *Dying for Ideas. The Dangerous Lives of the Philosophers* (2014). He has written for such publications as the *New York Times*, *The New Statesman*, *Dissent*, and *Times Literary Supplement*.

Philosophy as a Literary Art

Making Things Up

Edited by
Costica Bradatan

Routledge
Taylor & Francis Group

LONDON AND NEW YORK

First published 2015
by Routledge
2 Park Square, Milton Park, Abingdon, Oxon, OX14 4RN, UK

and by Routledge
711 Third Avenue, New York, NY 10017, USA

Routledge is an imprint of the Taylor & Francis Group, an informa business

British Library Cataloguing in Publication Data
A catalogue record for this book is available from the British Library

ISBN: 978-1-138-79244-9

Typeset in Bembo
by RefineCatch Ltd, Bungay, Suffolk

Publisher's Note
The publisher accepts responsibility for any inconsistencies that may have
arisen during the conversion of this book from journal articles to book chapters,
namely the possible inclusion of journal terminology.

Disclaimer
Every effort has been made to contact copyright holders for their permission to
reprint material in this book. The publishers would be grateful to hear from any
copyright holder who is not here acknowledged and will undertake to rectify
any errors or omissions in future editions of this book.

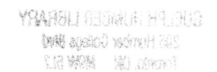

Contents

Citation Information

The chapters in this book were originally published in *The European Legacy*. When citing this material, please use the original page numbering for each article, as follows:

Chapter 1
Introduction: Unorthodox Remarks on Philosophy as Literature
Costica Bradatan
The European Legacy, volume 14, issue 5 (August 2009) pp. 513–518

Chapter 2
Of Poets and Thinkers. A Conversation on Philosophy, Literature and the Rebuilding of the World
Costica Bradatan, Simon Critchley, Giuseppe Mazzotta and Alexander Nehamas
The European Legacy, volume 14, issue 5 (August 2009) pp. 519–534

Chapter 3
Hunting Plato's Agalmata
Matthew Sharpe
The European Legacy, volume 14, issue 5 (August 2009) pp. 535–547

Chapter 4
The Nexus of Unity of an Emerson Sentence
Kelly Dean Jolley
The European Legacy, volume 14, issue 5 (August 2009) pp. 549–560

Chapter 5
The Concept of Writing, with Continual Reference to "Kierkegaard"
Mark Cortes Favis
The European Legacy, volume 14, issue 5 (August 2009) pp. 561–572

Chapter 6
An Inhumanly Wise Shame
Brendan Moran
The European Legacy, volume 14, issue 5 (August 2009) pp. 573–585

Chapter 7
Stanley Cavell and Two Pictures of the Voice
Adam Gonya
The European Legacy, volume 14, issue 5 (August 2009) pp. 587–598

Chapter 8
Philosophy, Poetry, Parataxis
Jonathan Monroe
The European Legacy, volume 14, issue 5 (August 2009) pp. 599–611

Chapter 9
Emphasising the Positive: The Critical Role of Schlegel's Aesthetics
James Corby
The European Legacy, volume 15, issue 6 (October 2010) pp. 751–768

Please direct any queries you may have about the citations to
clsuk.permissions@cengage.com

Notes on Contributors

Costica Bradatan, The Honors College, Texas Tech University, USA

James Corby, English Department, University of Malta, Malta

Simon Critchley, The New School, New York, USA

Mark Cortes Favis, Department of Philosophy, University of Essex, UK

Adam Gonya, The Institute of Philosophy, Catholic University of Leuven, Belgium

Kelly Dean Jolley, Department of Philosophy, Auburn University, USA

Giuseppe Mazzotta, Department of Italian, Yale University, USA

Jonathan Monroe, Department of Comparative Literature, Cornell University, USA

Brendan Moran, Faculty of Humanities, University of Calgary, Canada

Alexander Nehamas, Department of Humanities and Comparative Literature, Princeton University, USA

Matthew Sharpe, School of International and Political Studies, Deakin University, USA

Introduction: Unorthodox Remarks on Philosophy as Literature

~ Costica Bradatan ~

la metafísica es una rama de la literatura fantástica
    —Jorge Luis Borges, Ficciones. El aleph. El informe de Brodie

Philosophy is best seen as a kind of writing. It is delimited, as is any literary genre, not by form or matter, but by tradition.
    —Richard Rorty, "Philosophy as a Kind of Writing: An Essay on Derrida"

Like novelists, historians or columnists, philosophers, too, are writers. They make sophisticated use of language, and employ—whether deliberately or not—specific rhetorical and stylistic devices, as well as certain repertoires of metaphors, images and symbols. As writers, philosophers also have to adjust their writing to specific audiences, tailor it to serve specific purposes, and strategically choose one genre over another, with all its rules, protocols, and constraints. In short, it is crucial for philosophers—if they are to persuade readers—to advance their ideas following certain aesthetic rules, rhetorical procedures and strategies of persuasion. This whole process, however, ends up affecting in a structural way the very meaning of what philosophers have to say, a fact which has led some authors who have reflected on this aspect of philosophizing to speak of—in Berel Lang's terms—"the literariness of philosophical texts"[1] as something indistinguishable from the philosophical substance and relevance of those texts. One cannot really single out the "form" of a philosophical text, leave it aside as irrelevant and focus only on the "content" of the text. One is inconceivable without the other: "*how* you say it" is an essential part of "*what* you say."

A writer's relationship to language, writing and the weaving together of narratives in general is always complex. The notion that we use language, just as we use a tool, to make things with, is not only simplistic but sometimes in fundamental respects utterly false. On the contrary, it often happens that it is language that uses us and we end up as a mere tool in language's service. As Heidegger has put it, although "man acts as though *he* were the shaper and master of language ... in fact *language* remains the master of man."[2] It might thus well be the case that—as often happens with writers—philosophers, too, go through experiences of a very special nature: sometimes, for example, they are so completely seduced by language that they almost lose themselves in the act of writing and come to utter whatever language compels them to; at other times they become so deeply

~

1

caught up in their own discourse that it becomes difficult for them to separate themselves from it: on such occasions they are not very different from those novelists who end up becoming characters in the narratives they are constructing.

The implication of this complex relationship to language is that a work of philosophy might well be regarded as a work of (literary) art, as an autonomous, self-sufficient world, in whose creation and "bringing into being" the author's personal vision, imagination, playfulness and inventiveness play a major role. A good philosophical text needs to have a captivating narrative in the same way a good piece of fiction needs to have a good "plot." The way a philosopher envisions an argument is thus not unlike the way in which a novelist envisions, for example, a crucial encounter between two characters in her novel: each of them has to follow certain rules of narrative construction and configuration. In both cases, a superior sense of "inner necessity" suggests both what to do and how to do it. This necessity is, in other words, of an aesthetic or representational nature. In this sense, *The Phenomenology of Spirit* is, in a fundamental way, much closer to *Hamlet* or *The Brothers Karamazov* than to, say, *On the Origin of Species* or *The Theory of Relativity*. The type of truth that a philosophical work seeks to advance lies precisely in its expression: more exactly, this truth is what emerges when a philosophical writing of this kind hits its readers in a compelling manner.

★

While in the philosophical literature produced in, say, France, Germany or Italy, the idea of philosophy as literature has been broadly accepted for a long time, in the English-speaking world things are quite different: here to say that philosophy is—or can be seen as—a form of literature is still a provocative statement. Many serious analytic philosophers, for example, will never forgive Richard Rorty for siding with that Trojan horse—brought into the American academia by literary scholars[3]—known by the name of Jacques Derrida.[4] (That Rorty, later in life, ended up teaching in a department of comparative literature must look to these philosophers like a just, if insufficient, punishment.) Leaving aside the preoccupations of literary scholars with philosophical texts, as we should, given the current issue's focus on "philosophy as literature" as understood by philosophers themselves[4]—mainstream Anglo-American philosophers have been reluctant, to put it mildly, to open up a real conversation about the "literariness" of philosophical texts, the crucial role that imagination, creation and creativity play in philosophy, as well as the deeper significance of the literary and rhetorical aspects of philosophizing.

Despite growing scholarly interest among philosophers in the relation between philosophy and literature generally, over the last few decades comparatively few studies have been published dealing more narrowly with the literary aspects of philosophical texts.[6] In the vast majority of cases literary works draw the attention of philosophers from various philosophical angles (ethical, aesthetical, argumentative, epistemological, etc.) rather than the other way around. This trend has become so prevalent in mainstream Anglo-American philosophy that it often seems to exhaust all possible meanings of the relation between philosophy and literature. A symptomatic example at hand is a recent collection of essays on "literary philosophers."[7] In this otherwise enlightening book, the "literary philosophers" in question are not, as one might naively expect, Kierkegaard, Heidegger, Emerson, Wittgenstein or Walter Benjamin, but three fiction writers: Borges, Calvino, and Eco. Although a more accurate term for these writers might be "philosophical story-tellers" or "metaphysical fiction writers,"[8] the volume's editors have not deemed such a distinction necessary: considering philosophy literarily is presumably so remote a possibility that there is no fear readers might take "literary philosophers" as referring in fact to some ... philosophers.

The relationship philosophy–literature is thus far too often taken to be "literature *as* philosophy" and very rarely, almost never, "philosophy *as* literature." It is as though philosophers, so bold when it comes to analyzing others' works, feel overwhelmed by a sudden timidity when it is their own turn to be scrutinized and shy away from any curious gaze. While it is perfectly legitimate for them to study the plot of a novel from a variety of philosophical angles, it would be utterly irrelevant to discuss, say, the role of metaphors or that of imagery in the genesis of a certain piece of philosophical writing. To read philosophy literarily is, as Lang has put it, "at best an irrelevance, at worst a distortion."[9]

It is precisely the frustration brought about by this sense of one-sidedness and inexplicable resistance that lies at the origin of this special issue. Above all, a consideration of what philosophers do from a literary perspective should be seen, at the most basic level, as a matter of self-knowledge, an exercise in self-examination. Philosophy has nothing to lose (but a host of stereotypes and commonplaces as well as, at times, an insufferable sense of superiority) by engaging in a serious process of literary self-analysis. On the contrary, such an exercise would most likely make philosophy more interesting, more sophisticated, stronger, funnier, more playful, more self-ironizing—above all more self-reflexive.[10] By *not* moving in this direction, philosophy places itself in the rather embarrassing position of not following what (at least from Socrates onward) has been deemed as the worthiest of all philosophical ideals: self-knowledge.

★

The following contributions are not meant in any way to exhaust the topic of "philosophy as literature," nor do they aim to have the "last word" in the debate. While they offer a series of provisional reflections and articulations on the "literariness" of philosophy as it reveals itself in a limited number of instances, no systematic attempt has been made to cover a particular historical period, school of thought, or set of literary techniques used by philosophers. On the contrary, a certain "essayistic" spirit (in Montaigne's sense) rules resolutely throughout over the collection's form and structure.

In the opening conversation that frames the issue's thematic, historical and philosophical concerns, I asked Simon Critchley, Giuseppe Mazzotta, and Alexander Nehamas a number of questions about the many ways in which we might understand "philosophy as literature": How is it that philosophers—a professional class that used to count among its ranks winners of the Nobel Prize for Literature—are somehow saddened today when they are complimented on the quality of their prose? What's the role of philosophy and philosophizing in the "creation of the self"? How can philosophy contribute to the "rebuilding" of the world? How can one make a convincing argument today that philosophy is not just about arguments?

The collection's first essay, Matthew Sharpe's "Hunting Plato's *Agalmata*," is dedicated to one of the most celebrated cases of a synthesis of philosophy and literature: Plato's *Symposium*. Sharpe's interpretation of Plato is an oblique one to the extent that he deliberately reads the *Symposium* through a Lacanian lens. Focusing on elements of imagery in Plato's text, Sharpe's analysis revolves around the significance of Socrates' famous "Silenus-like language and appearance," behind which "there were *agalmata* [treasures] hidden in his belly." It is precisely this (ironically iconic) representation of Socrates that should offer us, in Sharpe's reading, the key to a deeper meaning of the Platonic philosophy as one that harbors "different levels of insight, couched in Plato's philosophy as literature." In the following essay, "The Nexus of Unity of an Emerson Sentence," Kelly Dean Jolley proposes a "phenomenology of reading Emerson," directing this phenomenological investigation, with the help of some insights from Frege, to an analysis of what exactly constitutes "the unity of an Emerson sentence." This unity, in its turn, is taken as the basis for a further exploration of what constitutes the unity of "the Emerson paragraph" and even of "the Emerson essay." As a case study for illustrating his findings, Jolley uses Emerson's essay "Experience."

In "The Concept of Writing, with Continual Reference to 'Kierkegaard'" Mark Cortes Favis explores the complex role of writing in Søren Kierkegaard's philosophy. Against what he sees as a prevalence of "Socratic" readings of Kierkegaard (with their emphasis on the "oral" quality of Kierkegaard's work), Favis focuses on Kierkegaard as a writer, an approach which allows him to position the Danish philosopher closer to Plato than to Socrates. Once the significance of "Kierkegaard the writer" has been established, the fascinating question is, of course: "if Kierkegaard's philosophy is really Socratic in nature, then how can he resemble such a 'pure thinker' who never wrote a single word?" The next essay, Brendan Moran's "An Inhumanly Wise Shame," documents Walter Benjamin as reader of Franz Kafka. According to Moran, Benjamin detects in Kafka's works "a gesture of shame" which he considers to be "historico-philosophic" (*geschichtsphilosophisch*). Where Kafka's gesture is philosophic "in opposing myth, which is closure concerning history," Benjamin's own analysis of this gesture comes to articulate itself, in its turn, as yet another "gesture of shame."

Adam Gonya's essay, "Stanley Cavell and Two Pictures of the Voice," starts out by distinguishing two "pictures of the voice": one that has to do with "deliberate conceptual performances," where we know what it is that we want to say and search for "the right word" (as exemplified in this case by Schopenhauer); and the other that has to do with "non-deliberate conceptual performance" (as exemplified by Nietzsche). Within this framework, Gonya examines in detail the differing ways in which Wittgenstein, Emerson, and Stanley Cavell respond to Shakespeare. Their responses amount for Gonya to articulated visions of the role of literature in philosophy and life. Finally, in "Philosophy, Poetry, Parataxis" Jonathan Monroe examines Giorgio Agamben as the paradigmatic case of a contemporary "literary philosopher" in whose work the poetic mode of language acquires new functions and plays a renewed role. Significantly, Monroe consistently positions Agamben's work not in relation to "professional" philosophers but in relation to poets (Charles Baudelaire, Paul Celan, Rosmarie Waldrop, and others) or to such similarly poetic philosophers as Walter Benjamin. What Monroe finds in the end "most symptomatic" about Agamben's writing is "the acuteness of the questions it asks in a global academic discursive economy" that is already a world where, in Benjamin's terminology, "the state of emergency" is not anymore "the exception but the rule, the habitual structure of radical inequity and injustice."

If there is one major theoretical claim that this issue makes in different ways and from various angles, it is the following: the literariness of philosophy is in an important sense a *philosophical* problem proper. While such literariness is clearly integral to the fields of literature, rhetoric, and literary theory, philosophers stand to lose more than merely one issue among others if they continue outsourcing it as a philosophically irrelevant, auxiliary concern with which only literary scholars should bother. If philosophers abandon literariness as a philosophical problem, they risk losing access to an important part of who they are.

★

This issue would not have been possible without the hard work, enthusiasm, intelligence, graciousness and generosity of many people. It delights me to offer special thanks here to all these people for bringing this project to fruition: the editors of *The European Legacy*, first of all for hosting the issue, but also for a very smooth editorial process and a wonderful collaboration; Simon Critchley, Giuseppe Mazzotta, and Alexander Nehamas, for their readiness to participate in the conversation that opens the issue, as well as for their fascinating insights, contagious conviviality, and great sense of humor; Jonathan Monroe for producing an excellent invited article in such a short time; the issue's other contributors: Matthew Sharpe, Kelly Dean Jolley, Mark Cortes Favis, Brendan Moran, and Adam Gonya, for all their hard work, talent, openness and patience; the anonymous reviewers of the numerous submissions to the issue, too many to list here but without whose dedication, hard work and generosity this issue would have never been possible; and finally, all those who showed interest and submitted papers for this special issue, including those whose submissions we were not able to include.

★

I dedicate this special issue to Professor Ion Ianoşi, my dearest teacher, from whom I learned almost everything I know about philosophy as literature.

Notes

1. This is a central notion in Berel Lang's The Anatomy of Philosophical Style: Literary Philosophy and the Philosophy of Literature (Oxford: Blackwell, 1990).
2. Martin Heidegger, *Poetry, Language, Thought*, trans. A. Hofstader (New York: Harper & Row, 1971), 146.
3. It is fully symptomatic for this state of affairs that Jacques Derrida was first introduced in the United States by literary scholars. Despite the fact that in France no one would question whether he was a philosopher or not, mainstream philosophers in the English-speaking world were for a long time quite sure that he was *not*. Moreover, to this day many philosophers here have made a strong point of seeing Derrida as someone having nothing to do with philosophy. With literary theory, comparative literature, French studies—maybe, but not with serious philosophy as they define it.
4. For more about the debate surrounding the reception of Derrida in America and how it shaped the philosophical landscape here, see Reed Way Dasenbrock, *Redrawing the Lines: Analytic Philosophy, Deconstruction, and Literary Theory* (Minneapolis, MN: University of Minnesota Press, 1989). For a recent general assessment of the scholarship dedicated to the relationship philosophy-literature (including philosophy as literature), see David Rudrum (ed.), *Literature and Philosophy. A Guide to Contemporary Debates* (Houndmills: Palgrave Macmillan, 2006).

5. However, I should add that this is only a provisional (and, to a certain extent, arbitrary) distinction, introduced here for the sake of simplicity. As a matter of fact, several materials in this issue engage (it would be impossible otherwise) with literary theory and scholarship. Moreover, some of the contributors to this issue are primarily literary scholars.   Even though they are only indirectly the object of this issue, let me just mention, by way of illustration, some of the most important contributions coming from literary studies: Harold Bloom, ed., *Deconstruction and Criticism* (London: Routledge, 1979); Paul de Man, *Allegories of Reading: Figural Language in Rousseau, Nietzsche, Rilke, and Proust* (New Haven, CT: Yale University Press, 1979). As examples of literary scholarship applied to discussing individual philosophers, see Peter Walmsley, *The Rhetoric of Berkeley's Philosophy* (Cambridge: Cambridge University Press, 1990), and Marjorie Perloff, *Wittgenstein's Ladder: Poetic Language and the Strangeness of the Ordinary* (Chicago, IL: University of Chicago Press, 1996).

6. One of the most prominent exceptions to this general state of affairs is, of course, Berel Lang, whose writings include, in addition to *The Anatomy of Philosophical Style, Philosophical Style: An Anthology about the Writing and Reading of Philosophy* (Chicago, IL: Nelson Hall, 1980), and *Philosophy and the Art of Writing: Studies and Philosophical and Literary Style* (Lewisburg, PA: Bucknell University Press, 1983). Along with Lang's works, which have made a tremendous contribution toward a serious consideration of philosophy from a literary point of view in the English-speaking world, other important exceptions include (in chronological order) Donald G. Marshall, ed., *Literature as Philosophy: Philosophy as Literature* (Iowa City, IA: University of Iowa Press, 1987); Anthony Cascardi, ed., *Literature and the Question of Philosophy* (Baltimore, MD: Johns Hopkins University Press, 1987); Jonathan Rée, *Philosophical Tales: An Essay on Philosophy and Literature* (London: Methuen, 1987); Martin Warmer, *Philosophical Finesse: Studies in the Art of Rational Persuasion* (Oxford: Clarendon Press, 1989); Stanley Cavell, *Philosophical Passages: Wittgenstein, Emerson, Austin, Derrida* (Oxford: Blackwell, 1995); Simon Critchley, *Very Little... Almost Nothing: Death, Philosophy, Literature* (London: Routledge, 1997); Andrew Benjamin, *Philosophy's Literature* (Manchester: Clinamen Press, 2001); David Rudrum, ed., *Literature and Philosophy: A Guide to Contemporary Debates* (Houndmills: Palgrave Macmillan, 2006).

7. Jorge J. E. Gracia, Karolyn Korsmeyer, and Rodolphe Gasché, eds., *Literary Philosophers: Borges, Calvino, Eco* (London: Routledge, 2002).

8. In the Introduction to the volume, Karolyn Kosrmeyer points out that the three writers are "as noted for the intriguing philosophical puzzles they present as they are for their inventive literary styles. These three authors are united not only by a taste for philosophy, but by their fascination with areas of philosophy not often broached in fiction: epistemology, metaphysics, and logic" (*Ibid.*, 2).

9. Lang, The Anatomy of Philosophical Style, 2.

10. Scholars in other humanistic disciplines have been doing this for a long time and, as a result, a whole range of fascinating topics and new methodological paths have opened up for them. In the field of history, for example, see Hayden White's crucial work *Metahistory: The Historical Imagination in Nineteenth Century Europe* (Baltimore, MD: Johns Hopkins University Press, 1974).

Addendum to Introduction

This volume reprints materials originally published in a special issue of *The European Legacy* (14:5, 2009) dedicated to "Philosophy as Literature." One essay has been added to those materials: "Emphasising the Positive: The Critical Role of Schlegel's Aesthetics," by James Corby, originally published in *The European Legacy*, 15:6, pp. 751–768. In his essay, James Corby, drawing on Fichte and Walter Benjamin, argues that Schlegel's notion of the *Wechselerweis* is meant to bridge the gap between the ideal and the real in "a positive experience of negation." Indeed, he argues that Schlegel's aesthetics is an attempt to articulate a "philosophico-literary form" that performs such bridging.

Of Poets and Thinkers: A Conversation on Philosophy, Literature and the Rebuilding of the World

～ Costica Bradatan, Simon Critchley, Giuseppe Mazzotta
and Alexander Nehamas ～

Sometimes there can be something supremely seductive about the unclear and the indistinct. On one occasion the ancient Chinese sage Chuang Chou made this disturbing confession, which must have left his disciples utterly perplexed: "Once Chuang Chou dreamt he was a butterfly, a butterfly flitting and fluttering around, happy with himself and doing as he pleased. He didn't know he was Chuang Chou. Suddenly he woke up and there he was, solid and unmistakable Chuang Chou. But he didn't know if he was Chuang Chou who had dreamt he was a butterfly, or a butterfly dreaming he was Chuang Chou" (trans. Burton Watson). The distinct philosophical charm of the situation Chuang Chou found himself in seems to come precisely out of the structural indistinctness on which it is based. Any attempt to pin it down would certainly spoil it; this charm exists only insofar as it remains related to the corresponding ambiguity. The only appropriate way to deal with such a situation consists precisely in "letting it be" and taking its indistinction as a given.

*In many respects, the relationship between philosophy and literature is not unlike that between Chuang Chou and the butterfly he was dreaming he was: its intense attractiveness comes precisely from the indistinctness on which it relies, and which, needless to say, is in itself a philosophical problem worthy of the most serious consideration. To discuss the charmingly ambiguous relationships between philosophy and literature I have invited three distinguished scholars of philosophy and literature: Simon Critchley, Professor and Chair of Philosophy at The New School for Social Research, Giuseppe Mazzotta, Sterling Professor in the Humanities for Italian at Yale University, and Alexander Nehamas, Carpenter Professor in the Humanities at Princeton University. (**C. B.**)*

★ ★ ★

Costica Bradatan: First of all, I would like to thank the three of you for kindly agreeing to take part in this conversation. I know how busy you all are and I am certainly grateful to you for finding the time to participate.

～

I would like to start with a certain observation that has puzzled me for some time. It is about a rather widespread presumption in today's mainstream philosophy (especially in the English-speaking world) that the literary aspects of a philosophical text do not in general mean anything, that they do not—and should not—play any significant role in the production, interpretation and appreciation of that text. It is as though a philosophical text is (or can be easily considered) something perfectly transparent, as if you can "see right through it," without having to take into account its literariness. The literariness of a philosophical text is, according to this prevalent view, perfectly negligible, something you can easily leave aside, and still the significance of that text will remain intact. There was a time, not long ago, when philosophers (a Bergson, for example) could get the Nobel Prize for Literature. Today, in some circles, if you praise philosophers for the literary qualities of their writings, they might well take that as a disguised criticism. How do you comment on this state of affairs? Where does it come from? What do you make of this trend?

Simon Critchley: Let me answer about the relation of philosophy to literature by telling a story. I remember having given a paper at the philosophy department of a prestigious English university that modesty forbids naming. I was in my late 20s and pretty inexperienced at giving papers. The question period was pretty lively and slightly hostile, I recall. At dinner afterwards, a philosopher of a rather different persuasion to mine said, in response to some remarks I'd made during questions, "I don't see why reading a philosopher isn't just like sitting down to dinner with him." The example we both had in mind was Descartes. I pointed out the fact that Descartes would probably not been fluent in English, lived 400 years ago in a very different and indeed explosive cultural and historical context, defined by the Thirty Years War in which was a participant, that he wrote in different styles in his Latin and vernacular texts and experimented constantly with literary form, using the Jesuitical meditation, Montaigne's autobiographical essay, and even allegedly finishing his career writing the verses to a ballet at the request of Queen Christina of Sweden. After I'd finished pleading, my interlocutor made the obvious move and said, "That's all very well from a historical and literary perspective, but what matters is the truth or falsity of Descartes' arguments."

The prejudice here is, as you say in your question, that we can read through the surface of a philosophical text and judge its arguments as either valid or invalid. The book series that epitomizes this approach is Routledge's "Arguments of the Philosophers," that I believe was first edited by Freddie Ayer, though I might be wrong. The presupposition of this approach is that it is only the arguments that are important and that we can ignore the historical, rhetorical, linguistic, cultural and literary features of a text as irrelevant surface details that are best ignored. I disagree very strongly with this approach. Arguments are obviously hugely important, but we ignore those other features at our peril and, when we do ignore them, we risk falling into a rather flat-footed philistine approach to philosophical texts. If philosophy is exclusively about arguments, then how do we explain the fact that there are so many poor arguments in so many philosophical texts, beginning with Plato's dialogues? Was Plato stupid?

I think we have reached a very peculiar state of affairs when philosophers are approached with suspicion because they write too well.

Alexander Nehamas: Analytical philosophy (I will limit myself to it here) is a Modernist movement—G. E. Moore was an inspiration to Bloomsbury; the Vienna Circle played an indispensable role in the intellectual turmoil following the First World War, its Berlin allies were part and parcel of Weimar Germany, and there is little need to list Wittgenstein's credentials. Modernism valued austerity, purity, and rigor; it avoided ornamentation; and it professed indifference to pleasing its audience, aiming at edifying it instead. It also took science to be the paradigmatic intellectual human accomplishment and saw itself as part of the scientific enterprise. And it found itself incorporated into an increasingly professionalized academic environment, to which a lingua franca, establishing among other things the credentials of its participants, was crucial. Put all these together and you begin to see some of the reasons why the literary aspects of writing have seemed irrelevant if not inimical to the enterprise of philosophy.

That is not to say that figures like Bertrand Russell or W. V. O. Quine were not talented writers; their writing, though, was not conventionally literary and—unlike, say, Wittgenstein's—it aimed more at suppressing their personality rather than at bringing it forward. Like the scientific paper and the legal brief or opinion, which have been by and large its models during much of the last century, philosophical writing aims at establishing truths that are as independent as possible from an author's particularities and idiosyncrasies. That sort of impersonality, which requires a style that effaces itself, allows scientific papers to describe experiments that can be repeated in different circumstances and legal texts to offer arguments that can be applied to cases quite distant from their original concerns.

A self-effacing style, however, is still a style: what it is not is an *individual* style. And it is, I think, the techniques that produce such a style, and not literary elements in general, that are regarded with suspicion in philosophy. Now I think that there are parts of philosophy where an impersonal approach has a place. It addresses problems that, as I have suggested, can be treated independently of the authors who present them because they are inherently general and are of little relevance to their authors' particular lives. What doesn't have a place, though, is the prejudice that only the impersonal approach is legitimate in addressing philosophical problems and, moreover, that only problems amenable to that sort of treatment are legitimate philosophical questions.

It is for these two reasons that it has been difficult (more in some cases, less in others) to find a place in the philosophical canon for figures like Montaigne, Pascal, Schopenhauer, Kierkegaard, Emerson, Nietzsche, and, again, Wittgenstein. In addition to addressing problems in metaphysics, epistemology or the philosophy of language, these philosophers seem aware that, when it comes to asking how life is to be lived— Socrates' question, surely a legitimate philosophical issue—the answer will depend on the particular individual who is asking the question. For the question is how to make life worthwhile, given the specific—and very different—features, needs, desires, and abilities that belong to each one of us as well as the vastly different situations of each individual. Since the answer to that question varies systematically depending on who is asking, the philosophers I am discussing often offer explicit or implicit self-portraits articulating their own answer, which cannot be anyone else's answer but may still, perhaps, inspire others to look *for their own answer* in turn.

I realize I haven't said anything about Descartes, who, as Simon Critchley so forcefully reminds us, developed a most personal style of his own, or about Plato, who seems to belong to both groups at the same time. But I don't want to make this longer than it already is; if anyone is interested, we can discuss them on another occasion. I also realize that the classifications I have offered here are crude and rough. These are issues with which I am occupied these days, and I am always most confused about what is uppermost in my mind.

Costica Bradatan: I think that Alexander Nehamas raises a fundamental meta-philosophical issue here. For, it seems to me, this all too vehement treatment of philosophy as not having anything to do with literature, deliberately ignoring the stylistic aspects of philosophizing, is in itself a, yes, *literary* option—one out of several possible. Writing "without style" is certainly a stylistic choice; the refusal of literature is a form of literature, just as iconoclasm betrays a certain type of aesthetic sensibility. Therefore, as Alexander Nehamas's genealogy suggests, the analytic philosophers' declaration of war against the literariness of philosophy could be construed as a *radical literary manifesto* of sorts. But, then, I cannot help noticing that analytic philosophers don't do that deliberately today, that usually it does not cross their minds that theirs too is a literary, stylistic choice. (When there is only one valid way of doing philosophy, you cannot speak of choice, can you?) Thus, most ironically, a discipline that was once founded on the maxim "know thyself," and has over the centuries made teaching people self-knowledge one of its fundamental concerns, ends up ignoring something important about its own nature.

Giuseppe Mazzotta: It is not at all clear that we can agree about what constitutes "literature," and the history of literary studies is notoriously marked by endless debates. In our times the prevailing trends have been New Criticism, Deconstruction, New Historicism, Cultural Studies, Gender studies etc. They all presuppose different views about the purposes of literature and its resistance to/complicity with the hegemony of political and social discourses and taste. With different degree of conviction, however, these critical currents all share a couple of concerns: literary language (the texts by Homer, Lucretius, Virgil, Dante, Machiavelli, Shakespeare, Cervantes, Goethe, Tolstoy, Proust etc.) is marked by creativity and by a high degree of self-reflexivity about language itself and its ambiguities.

I myself am strongly drawn to philosophers/thinkers who grasp the basic questions put forth by the literary texts (Vico or Nietzsche, Emerson or Cavell) and they range from questions about authority and the self to issues such as knowledge (or non-knowledge), imagination, and representation, truth and fiction and the value of human experience, and dilemmas about beliefs and trust etc. An unavoidable dialogue or monologues of misunderstanding exists between the two institutional forms of thought. Within the academic institutions, in effect, a barrier of suspicions has been traditionally erected by philosophers toward literary studies and by literary scholars toward philosophers.

Philosophers' suspicions may in part have to do, I fear, with the way a number of literary scholars engage themselves with philosophical problems. The literary critics who "do" philosophy from within literary studies act as if impelled to make the reading of novels "relevant" to our times. In the process they rush to find in literary texts the most up-to-date formulations by Lacan, Derrida, Foucault etc. and lose sight of the specificity of their own disciplines. On the other hand, philologists themselves tend to be skeptical of and to reject all philosophical claims by literature.

Costica Bradatan: I am very grateful to Giuseppe Mazzotta for this framing of the issue of "philosophy as literature" in terms of literary studies. It is crucial, I think, to embrace this topic from different angles and place it in a broader interdisciplinary perspective.

Here is my next question: if, as we seem to have agreed, philosophy is not "just about arguments," but is something more complex than that, then it would be worth articulating a better and more comprehensive understanding of what philosophy is. I mean, specifically, an understanding that incorporates the issues of rhetoric and style, of imagination and "poeticity," the structural role of metaphors, the fundamental function of expression and expressivity. Not that something like this hasn't been done before. In fact, it would be legitimate, I think, to talk about a tradition of philosophers who have recurrently come up with such articulations. Vico and Nietzsche, to give only a couple of isolated examples, made the case vigorously for a "poetic philosophy," for a philosophy rooted in the notions of imagination and creation. However, it seems that every generation has to do this thing for itself, to start everything anew. Considering that in many contemporary philosophical circles to say "poetic philosophy" would be like saying "square circle," how can one make a convincing case for a literary philosophy today? If you were to talk about it to a reticent—perhaps slightly hostile—audience, how would you explain why it would be a good idea to operate with this more comprehensive notion of philosophy? What is to be gained from it? In short, how would you make an argument today that philosophy is not just about arguments?

Giuseppe Mazzotta: I think the institutional gap between "literature" and "philosophy" is actually a secondary problem. The conception of literature as concerned with the inquiry into/representation of the meaning of the self, a life, one's possible selves or possible worlds, carries with it the conception of a new way of philosophizing and, thereby, altering fixed ideas or fictions of abstract philosophical coherence. The relation—often viewed as a quarrel—between literature and philosophy has always been circular—with echoes and resonances of one in the other (notions of signs, time, place, history, love, power, beauty, deceptions, madness, death or what Alexander calls "Style" as the mode of individualization etc.). One cannot but experience a back and forth movement between different registers and discourses, and, in this sense, the end of traditional philosophy, announced by Heidegger, has already taken place. It is replaced by the most ancient form of openness in asking and answering. It is a mode that aims at expanding our life-horizon.

The way the academic institutions can respond to this shift in the way we have come to understand a work of art as productive of signs and truths is probably by re-proposing something like a new encyclopaedism, a sense of the conversation within the plurality of disciplines, each of which can exist as separate, fragmentary entities, and none of which can be thought of as autonomous and complete. The question of how to bring about the crossing of contiguous limits and borders would remain. Literature and philosophy, in their different ways, take us to the limit, there where the law is and where we are asked to define, re-define and test those limits. Had we enough space and time, we probably would have to invoke the faculty of the imagination as the force that brings about associations and dissociations. The passion for sharing and communicating is located in the fictions and utopias of the imagination (which, as we all know, is neither illusory nor real).

Alexander Nehamas: I would like to begin by repeating something I said in my last communication. I am not really comfortable with the idea that philosophy and literature should be sharply contrasted, at least in part because "literature" is not a purely descriptive category: it is also at least in part evaluative, and to consider something as literature is, to some extent, to praise it (although we also apply the term to texts that aspire to be considered as such, even if they are of minor importance). Many philosophical texts are in that sense literary: Descartes, Hume, Russell, and Quine—among others—would certainly qualify as literary authors. For me, the difference is not between philosophy and literature (and Giuseppe Mazzotta is right to insist that we can't easily agree on what counts as literature) but between writing that aspires to impersonality and writing that allows its author a strong individual presence, sometimes almost an intrusion. For the same reasons, I am wary of the term "poetical."

To the extent that I am right, it follows that there is a place for both personal and impersonal approaches within philosophy itself—some philosophy may well be just about arguments (although, I believe, to think that only arguments are legitimate philosophical considerations is to take too narrow a view of what counts as philosophy). The problem, as things are today, is with the idea that personal writing can't be philosophical. But because that idea is not based on purely intellectual considerations (it also depends on institutional ones as well)—for instance, the history of analytical philosophy and the intellectual orientation of many of those who have been attracted to it—it is not easy to give "an argument" that philosophy is not only about arguments.

One way to approach the issue is to offer an interpretation of the personal writing of a philosopher that connects with the interests of those who favor an exclusively argumentative approach. But the danger here is that such interpretations may end up ignoring the personal element altogether and end up attributing flat-footed or banal ideas to the philosophers involved; they then invite the response, "Well, if *that* is what X is trying to say, it's no news to us—and it could have been said much more straightforwardly." So, to the extent that the personal approach is relevant to the ideas expressed, it is important to note its effect on their texture and to making a point of addressing it directly.

Another approach, perfectly compatible with the first, is to suggest that what characterizes philosophical writing in general is a commitment to providing reasons for one's views, and that not every reason has to be an argument. To think that it does, I think, is to trivialize the idea of an argument: constructing a (verbal) picture of what it would be like to accept certain philosophical views, and offering that picture for inspection—as Nietzsche, for one, often does—seems to me to be a way of providing a reason for (or, for some, against!) accepting those views. But such a reason is not strictly speaking an argument, for whether one finds the picture attractive or not depends, on Nietzsche's own account, not just on the picture's content but also on the kind of person one is. And, short of being crudely uninformative (A is "healthy/strong," B is "sick/weak") there is no way of giving a description of the kind of person one is in terms specific enough to allow us to say something like "If you are such-and-such a person, you will find the picture attractive; if not, not," and use it, that is, as a premise of an argument.

I realize that this is both vague and not a direct answer to Costica's question but I hope it stays within the range of the issues we are discussing.

Costica Bradatan: I am sorry if I've made things even less clear than they were before. "Poetic" can indeed mean many things. Actually, when I used "poetic philosophy" I was rather toying with the title of one of Giuseppe's books (*The New Map of the World: The Poetic Philosophy of Giambattista Vico*).

Simon Critchley: I'd like to take up two issues, one raised by Costica and Giuseppe Mazzotta and the other by Alexander Nehamas. The first concerns the idea of "poetic philosophy." Let me begin anecdotally.

I do not write poetry. T. S. Eliot says somewhere that the only poets to be taken seriously are those who write after the age of 25. I stopped writing poetry at 24, largely as a consequence of reading Auden. He seemed to be able to say whatever it was that I wanted to say in whatever form he chose. I decided to throw in the towel. As a consequence, I became an ardent reader of poetry. My poetic passions waxed and waned, but the poet I came to be obsessed with was Wallace Stevens. I think that Stevens's poetry, in particular his long, late, meditative poems, like "An Ordinary Evening in New Haven," decisively recast what is arguably the fundamental concern of philosophy, namely the relation between thought and things, mind and world or, in Steven's parlance, imagination and reality. But what is crucial is that they cast it in poetic form, as a poem. When Stevens attempted to write philosophy, which he did in a paper called "A Collect of Philosophy," the results were, at best, uneven, and I believe the paper was rejected by *Mind*, and rightly so. What Stevens was able to develop was a unique meditative voice that used poetic form in order to develop full thoughts: theses, hypotheses ("if" was probably Stevens's favorite word), ruminations and aphorisms that one should call philosophical.

A couple of consequences follow from this:

1. I don't think that what Stevens was doing could be described as "poetic philosophy" (or even "philosophical poetry," although that is closer to the truth). It is poetry concerned with an issue (the relation between mind and world, say) that is also of concern to philosophers. But the form of expression is vitally different and that difference has to be respected.

2. This raises the issue as to how one writes about poetry as a philosopher. Giuseppe Mazzotta puts his finger on a loathsome tendency, which is the *use* of poetry or literature to confirm usually half-digested gobbets of Lacan, Derrida or whoever. This is poetry reduced to the status of an example to illustrate some theory. I think the procedure should be precisely reversed. It is not a question of using a theory to explain a poem simply in order to confirm that theory. Nor is it a matter of paraphrasing or explaining somehow obscure poetic utterance in clear philosophical form. It is rather a question of trying to read a poet carefully in order to point towards an experience of mind, language and world that is best expressed poetically. The entire difficulty consists in the nature of that pointing towards: how does one write about poetry as a philosopher in a way that does not drown the poem in concepts alien to its mode of utterance. In this sense, it is not a question of 'poetic philosophy' as much as a philosophical attempt to convey an

experience of thinking that takes place poetically. This requires something like 'tact.'

The second issue concerns the question of impersonality versus personality in philosophy and Alexander Nehamas's description of the contemporary suspicion of a personal style in philosophical writing. I would like to link this to the effects of professionalization on philosophy. As we all know, it was a commonplace in antiquity, and long after antiquity, to hold that philosophy was something transformative or disruptive of what it means to be a self. As Hadot has it, philosophy was a way of life. As a consequence, it was hard, in the case of a Socrates or an Epicurus to draw the line between philosophy and life. I would argue that the appeal of thinkers like Nietzsche, Heidegger, Arendt or Foucault is not just that some of these thinkers led interesting lives, but that they are thinkers for whom philosophy had a transformative effect, an effect that lives on in their readers.

Costica Bradatan: How does this relate to the question of professionalization?

Simon Critchley: In his book on Edith Stein, Alasdair MacIntyre writes,

> Imprisoning philosophy within the professionalizations and specializations of an institutionalized curriculum, after the manner of our contemporary European and North American culture, is arguably a good deal more effective in neutralizing its effects than either religious censorship or political terror.

The effect of the professionalization of philosophy is the sense that it does not and should not matter to the conduct of one's life. Philosophy should aspire to the impersonality of natural science. Nothing more. Philosophy is a technically complex academic discipline with its own internal criteria of excellence and it should be kept away from other humanistic disciplines and from the unseemly disorder of private and public lives. This is the view that I'd like to challenge.

Incidentally, there are philosophers who powerfully adopt a personal style in their writing, like Nietzsche. But there are also philosophers who adopt a highly impersonal style, which is rightly linked to modernism as Alexander Nehamas points out, as for example in the early Wittgenstein. But the personal style of Nietzsche and the impersonal style of Wittgenstein are both forms of address that are intended to have a profound existential effect on their readers. Then there are philosophers, like Ayer, who would draw a radical distinction between philosophy, understood as conceptual analysis, and "all of life," as Ayer said to Berlin in the 1930s. I suppose what I object to are those philosophers who don't care about the existential dimension of philosophical writing.

Excuse the length of this response. I'm not sure if it clears the water or muddies it.

Costica Bradatan: I am glad that both Alexander Nehamas and Simon Critchley have brought up the topic of philosophy as an art of living because my next question is going to be about something closely related to this topic: the "creation of the self." With a history that goes back as far as, say, Socrates, the notion that the self is not something we are born with, but something we constantly create and recreate is one of the favorite topics of philosophical modernity. I know that each one of you has worked—or at least touched—on this topic in your works. In *The New Map of the World* Giuseppe Mazzotta examines the presence of the topic in Vico, for whom "there is no a priori essence for the self: one is what one makes of oneself, and one makes of oneself what one knows, so that being, knowledge, and making are ceaselessly interwoven in an endless recirculation" (27). In a certain sense, the self of an author is the result of the books he writes; the books that Vico wrote made him who he was, they "wrote" him in a way: "the *New Science* makes him, gives him authority, at least as much as he makes the *New Science*" (18). It would, therefore, be legitimate to speak of "a history of the self" in Vico, of a self structurally caught up in the logic of historicity, or, as Giuseppe puts it, a "*subjectum* . . . literally thrown under, without a firm foundation, losing control of oneself, and provisionally without consciousness" (19). To regain control of one's self, to put it on its feet, is a lifetime's project. The one who embarks on such a major project has something of the artist in the pursuit of *magnum opus*. The process of creating a unique self for oneself thus becomes a very difficult and demanding art (in *La Gaya Scienza* Nietzsche exclaims: "to 'give style' to one's character—a great and rare art"!). At the limit, even one's death can be employed in one's project of fashioning a self. As Simon Critchley puts it in his *Very Little . . . Almost Nothing*, "individual authenticity produces itself through acts of self-invention and self-creation, where death becomes my work and suicide becomes the ultimate possibility—*ergo* the logical suicide of Kirilov" (25).

Now, if we decide to see the creation of the self as the central purpose of a lifetime's project, then philosophy—in charge as it is of the "care of the self"—comes to acquire some of the characteristics of this creative project: it becomes, in its turn, a *creative* activity (in this sense we can probably speak of a "poietic philosophy"). As such, seen from this particular angle, the topic of our special issue—philosophy as literature—becomes of increased importance. The link between the two is not something accidental, but something grounded in a broader vision of the human condition and its ontology. Accordingly, the philosopher who adopts the view that the creation of the self should be our most important task is not unlike an author of fiction, someone whose job is to create "characters," to multiply "selves." This is one of the central points that Alexander Nehamas makes in his book *The Art of Living*. The creation of the self is, for him, equally a literary and a philosophical accomplishment: "It is a philosophical accomplishment because the content and nature of the self created in the process . . . depends on holding views on issues that have traditionally been considered philosophical. . . . It is literary because the connection between those philosophical views is not only a matter of systematic logical interrelations but also, more centrally, a matter of style" (3). In this "aestheticist" perspective, to create a self" is to succeed in becoming *someone*, in becoming a *character*, that is, someone unusual and distinctive" (4). As a result, "the philosophers of the art of living" that Alexander talks about in his book (Foucault, Nietzsche), as well as those whom he only mentions in passing (Pascal, Schopenhauer, Kierkegaard, Emerson, Thoreau, and, "on one reading at least," Wittgenstein) are, at the same time, figures usually considered whenever the topic of "philosophy as literature" comes up.

In light of these (maybe a little too long) considerations, a fundamental question arises, which I am proposing for discussion: if the chief task of philosophy is to participate in a literary "creation of the self," what would be the role of such (preeminently) literary notions as narration, genre, authorial point of view, tropes, plot, in the production of a philosophical discourse?

I am of course aware that this is a rather broad question, and that it is difficult in this conversation to go anywhere beyond a basic mapping out of a very complex territory.

Alexander Nehamas: I certainly agree with Costica that "creation of the self" is, if not *the* chief, among the chief tasks of philosophy. It is also among the chief tasks of other practices and disciplines and, anyway, philosophy has room for many other projects, which have little to do directly with self-creation. The main point for me, though, is that—as I have tried to suggest in our discussion so far—the relevant contrast is not primarily between a literary and a non-literary kind of philosophy. All philosophy is in a broad sense literary in so far as it is written. But some philosophy is written in what I have called a personal style and some, in a style that aspires to impersonality. It is true that in *The Art of Living*—in the very passage that Costica cites in his question—I do appeal to "literature," but I have come to think that this was an error.

Further, on my understanding, not every philosopher with a distinctive, personal style takes what I call an "aestheticist" approach to self-creation. For example, in his "middle" and "late" works (everything other that his Socratic dialogues, which are, to say the least, ambiguous), Plato presents a self (he calls it "Socrates" or "the philosopher") that he believes is profoundly true to human nature in general. Accordingly, he offers it as a model of emulation for everyone: to the extent that one fails to live up to it, one fails as a human being. In contrast, aestheticist philosophers present themselves as characters that can't be directly emulated: to attempt such a thing would result—to the extent that it could be at all successful—in producing a copy of their original. But that would be to miss altogether the point of their work, which is to offer themselves as inspiration for others to fashion selves *of their own*, on the basis of their particular circumstances, which are different for each individual and for that reason make direct imitation of another ultimately impossible.

In any case, the short answer to Costica's final question seems to me to be that it is not possible to state in general terms the role of various literary devices in a philosophical project of self-creation—no more, that is, than it is possible to make such a general statement about any literary genre. For example, Robert Browning's "A Grammarian's Funeral Shortly after the Revival of Learning in Europe," part of which I cite below, depends crucially on metaphors of height and depth, light and night, mountains and valleys, city and country, in order to establish the respect and admiration of the grammarian's students:

> Let us begin and carry up this corpse,
> Singing together.
> Leave we the common crofts, the vulgar thorpes
> Each in its tether
> Sleeping safe on the bosom of the plain,
> Cared-for till cock-crow:
> Look out if yonder be not day again
> Rimming the rock-row!
> That's the appropriate country; there, man's thought,
> Rarer, intenser,
> Self-gathered for an outbreak, as it ought,
> Chafes in the censer.
> Leave we the unlettered plain its herd and crop;
> Seek we sepulture
> On a tall mountain, citied to the top,

Crowded with culture!
All the peaks soar, but one the rest excels;
Clouds overcome it;
No! yonder sparkle is the citadel's
Circling its summit.
Thither our path lies; wind we up the heights:
Wait ye the warning?
Our low life was the level's and the night's;
He's for the morning.
Step to a tune, square chests, erect each head,
'Ware the beholders!
This is our master, famous, calm and dead,
Borne on our shoulders.

C. P. Cavafy, though, addressing a surprisingly similar theme in "Tomb of the Grammarian Lysias," does without metaphor or any obvious literary trope:

In the library of Beirut, just to the right as you go in,
we buried the wise Lysias, the grammarian.
The spot is most appropriate.
We placed him near those things of his
that he perhaps remembers even there:
notes, texts, commentaries, variants,
all kinds of studies of Greek idioms.
Also, this way, as we pass on our way to the books,
we'll see and honor his tomb.
(trans. Edmund Keeley and Philip Sherrard, modified)

I realize this is but one puny example, but the general point seems to me undeniable: no such generalizations are possible.

Costica Bradatan: How about, then, the "creation" of the self?

Alexander Nehamas: Let me turn to an issue raised through the statement by Giuseppe Mazzotta that Costica cites in his question, to the effect that the self of an author is the result of the books he writes and that the books Vico, in particular, wrote made him who he was, that in a way they "wrote" him: "*The New Science* makes him, gives him authority, at least as much as he makes the *New Science*." I think that is exactly right. But I am also conscious of the fact that many people are convinced that a huge gap exists between "the work" and "the life," philosophy and actuality—a gap that isolates the philosophy of self-creation in a realm of pure speculation and deprives it of any significance beyond its theoretical content.

This danger may seem clearest in Nietzsche's case. Nietzsche, who once wrote that "if you compare Kant and Schopenhauer with Plato, Spinoza, Pascal, Rousseau, Goethe in respect of their soul and not of their mind, then the former are at a disadvantage: their thoughts do not constitute a passionate history of the soul; there is nothing here that would make a novel, no crises, catastrophes or death-scenes; their thinking is not at the same time an involuntary biography of a soul," took his own work to be nothing but a "passionate history of his soul." But Nietzsche, as we know, led a life—modest, unhappy, and unfulfilled; plagued by illness, loneliness, and lack of recognition—that has seemed to most people depressingly different from the life praised in his writings and which he finally claims as his own in *Ecce Homo*. In fact, it is still common to take the headings of that book's sections—"Why I Am so Wise," for instance, or "Why I Am a Destiny"—simply as signs of his incipient madness. Think of Miguel de Unamuno, who characterized Nietzsche's philosophy as "the doctrine of weaklings who aspire to be strong," and saw Nietzsche himself as exactly the type, "slave," against whom *On the Genealogy of Morality* was written. Or consider that a contemporary American author finds him so sad and pitiful that he confesses he "wouldn't wish the life that Nietzsche lived on anyone, not even Rousseau"! I must confess that I too expressed a view of that sort in my book on Nietzsche when I separated "the man" from "the work" and claimed that "in engaging with his works, we are not engaging with the miserable little man who wrote them but with the philosopher who emerges through them, the magnificent character these texts constitute and manifest the agent who, as the will to power holds, is nothing but his effects—that is, his writings."

But that is a terrible mistake. The distinction between "the miserable little man" and "the magnificent philosopher"—"the man" and "the work"—requires us to think of "the life" as everything that is part of someone's biography *except for his work*! That, in turn, is to think of "the man" as the person who produced the work in isolation from that work, as if one's work is a less important part of life than the bills, the meals and the casual conversations, the illnesses and disappointments that are its inevitable accompaniments. It is an even worse mistake when "the man," like Nietzsche and the philosophers we are discussing here, is so devoted to "the work" that he subordinates the rest of his life to it. No—the work of a philosopher is an integral part of his life: you could not "wish the life that Nietzsche lived" on someone else without necessarily giving that person the most important part of Nietzsche's life: his own philosophy. That, I think, is what Giuseppe's statement brings so clearly to our attention.

Costica Bradatan: I must apologize to Alexander for going back, again and again, to the same things and pivoting around the same topic of philosophy as literature. It looks like the topic of this issue that I am editing must have ended up becoming an obsession for me. Most likely, this issue has in its turn started "editing" me.

What particularly attracted me to the notion of a "literary" creation of the self (as presented by Giuseppe in his book on Vico and by Alexander in *The Art of Living*) was precisely the implied promise that the "miserable" self, with all its meals and bills, with its boring daily routine, can be somehow "dissolved" into the "magnificent" self. If this were not too big a word, one could say that the latter can under certain circumstances "redeem" the former. If I am not mistaken, this is a lesson we can draw from one of Borges's short stories. (I am sure you all know the story, but it is worth recalling here.) This text, which in the Spanish original bears an English title (*Everything and Nothing*), is about Shakespeare's quest for a self, for himself, and in the end it is about Shakespeare's death. This short story (which starts with: "There was no one in him . . ."), ends with the following statement: "History adds that before or after he died, he discovered himself standing before God, and said to Him: *I who have been so many men in vain, wish to be one, to be myself.* God's voice answered him out of a whirlwind: *I, too, am not I; I dreamed the world as you, Shakespeare, dreamed your own work, and among the forms of my dreams are you, who like me are many, yet no one."*

I am aware that this does not do much to address Alexander's point about the need to really care for that self caught up in the trifles of everyday life, but at least it points to a slightly different perspective. If we don't seem to be much, we should not be too concerned about that: just like God, we have this peculiar ability of being *mucho y nadie* at the same time.

Giuseppe Mazzotta: There is one phrase in Alexander Nehamas's response that I found particularly striking. Alexander is addressing the "gap" that seems to emerge between "the work" and "the life" of an author, "philosophy" and "actuality," and this gap "relegates" the question of philosophical self-creation to the realm of pure abstraction. He goes on to argue quite convincingly about the error of separating life from works.

The phrase crystallizes for me what has been going on in our conversation, including even the concerns with disciplinary structures, the border between philosophy (or literature) and life, and philosophy and literature, amply discussed by Simon and Alexander. The analogies between ways of thinking about the self and arguments that literature has long died (or t the "end of man"), and between the way we conceive (and worry over) the fragmentation of our disciplines, or wonder about the particular commitment to our field are transparent.

I value highly the mere desire of making literature and philosophy insert themselves into our lives, and at a gut level think Heidegger's (and Foucault's and Derrida's) claims about the "end of man" both absurd and interesting. What these phrases—end of man, end of literature—intimate, is the need to reconstruct our worlds, to reconceptualize the idea of "our" world, an activity which I find prior to finding the place of the self in the world.

The metaphor of the "gap" recalls, properly speaking, a divergence or hiatus rather than a border, something difficult and maybe impossible to achieve for one's life and works or disciplines. Even if we promote ideals of communication within or unification of humanity we cannot really cancel borders, fill gaps or find the ultimate truth about oneself. It follows that we can think about the self (or the compartmentalizing of disciplines and, for that matter, of nations of the world) by exposing the fragmentary and incomplete nature of our being.

Both Simon and Alexander rightly insist that philosophy needs to think from the perspective of the non-place of literature and "translate" that thought into a multiplicity of other languages and styles. All of this may simply mean the gap may help us identify our place in the world.

Costica Bradatan: I would like to take up Giuseppe's suggestion and focus the next question on this notion of "reconstruction" of the world. This is in fact an idea that has been the subject of several of Giuseppe's books (of *The New Map of the World*, which I already mentioned, as well as of *Cosmopoiesis* and of *The World at Play*), and I am proposing it now because there seems to be some common thematic ground here: both Simon and Alexander have, in their specific ways, dealt with, or at least touched on, this issue in their works. For—if I am not completely mistaken—what Simon does in his *Infinitely Demanding* is a "rebuilding" of the political world through an "ethics of commitment," just as what Alexander does in *Only a Promise of Happiness* may be seen, in a sense, as a "reconstruction" of the world through a recovery of the notion of beauty. Therefore, I would like to propose for discussion the relation between philosophy, literature and the "rebuilding" of the world.

Simon Critchley: For my sins, I am teaching the whole of Heidegger's *Being and Time* this semester and on Tuesday I tried to lay out his concept of world in terms of the categorial distinction he advances between the ready-to-hand and the present-at-hand, or the handy, usefully pragmatic and the theoretical beholding of things as objects over against a subject. Obviously, Heidegger favors the former over the latter. But subtending both categories is his claim that *Dasein* is the worldhood of the world, namely that the human being is the a priori condition of possibility for there being a world at all. This culminates in what I see (others disagree) as the idealist thesis that there would be no world without *Dasein*, or no world without a self for whom that world was such and such.

Whatever one makes of this claim, I think this position is even more powerfully articulated by Walllace Stevens in "The Idea of Order at Key West," which is a meditation on the nature of the process of poetic creation. It is a conversation poem in the Coleridgean style, were two figures, Ramon Fernandez and the poetic voice, the 'we' who observe a figure referred to simply as "she.' Stevens writes,

> She was the single artificer of the world
> In which she sang. And when she sang, the sea,
> Whatever self it had, became the self
> That was her song, for she was the maker. Then we,
> As we beheld her striding there alone,
> Knew that there never was a world for her
> Except the one she sang, and singing, made.

Sometimes, I think this is just right. It's certainly beautiful. Words of the world are the life of the world and we make a world in words or build a world as Costica asks. Remove those words, namely remove us, and there is no meaningful world.

But then again, the problem that it raises is how to deal with a "subject"-independent reality: raw, brute physical nature, all 13 billion years of it. On my reading, this is the problem that Stevens grapples with in his late poems, for example in "Not ideas about the thing, but the thing itself." Namely, how can we begin to conceive of the thing itself, of nature *pur et dur*? I think this draws Stevens—and some other poets too, I think of Pessoa—towards a kind of anti-poetry, a poetics of a material reality that poetry cannot grasp . . .

Are we condemned to drift between idealism and realism without end? Many philosophers have believed that they have settled this question. I remain skeptical.

Giuseppe Mazzotta: Almost every significant thinker over roughly the last fifty years has tried to give a more or less explicit reinterpretation of the notion of the "world," from the familiar world in which we find ourselves to the public world we share—the world as a context of shared signification. One can think of Heidegger's sense of the "world," Marxist utopias, and Enlightenment schemes about freedom. Come to think of it, this genre goes back to Plato's utopia and the Renaissance updating of that myth

(More, Campanella, Bacon etc. with their insights on perspective and on how space can be manipulated), and they all seek to come to grips with old aristocratic models or simply strip existing values of their accretions.

Paraphrasing Marx, one can say that, more than interpreting the world, many recent thinkers/scholars have tried to re-conceive one aspect of the "world": the question of limits or borders. The assumption behind this direction of thought is that the world is not a static conception or place. A place can be transformed and can be scientifically constructed. A fairly dramatic recent case of such an emerging configuration of "world" is A. Negri's *Empire* (a mixture of Marxist, Spinozist and Deleuzeian utopias) in which he actually imagines a world without borders. No possible transgression can exist in such a picture of the world, and, in effect, Negri completely brackets the potentially tragic aspect of this fantasy: a world without limits or borders can be easily thought of as engendering the chaos and devastating violence tragic texts steadily reveal. The Biblical myth of Babel's confusion of languages is a pointed metaphor of this possibility.

For the most part, however, the ongoing re-conceptualization of the world focuses on all limits, questions them, and re-negotiates them. The limits concern the sexes (and the borders within each of them), countries, social classes, languages, religions, ethics (human beings and animals), the relation between the arts and sciences, literature and philosophy etc. Contrary to what one might think (I have often thought disparagingly of my own discipline), literary studies have moved to the forefront of these concerns (especially gender theories and neo-historicism). Latin American and Indian-English novels have inaugurated the mode. Benjamin's theory of translation (or Derrida's "difference"), to mention a couple of examples, show the philosophers' will to clarify our practices and beliefs.

Whether or not a "global" understanding emerges from these critical reflections is necessarily a moot question. And limits (political, religious, biological etc.) keep imposing themselves.

Alexander Nehamas: Here is a completely irresponsible gesture, a reaction not primarily to Costica's question but to Simon's moving reply. Perhaps to say that there would be no world without a subject is not to slide into idealism, if we take "the world" to be not "brute nature" but the physical/cultural/social/conceptual space within which we live our actual lives. That world (I won't even pretend that I know Heidegger well enough to attribute the view to him, though it sounds right) is a joint product of whatever the universe is like and the interactions of human beings with that universe. But there was no first moment when the universe was turned into a world: the world was always already there, like culture, society, and language. So the interaction is always between human beings and the world in which we find ourselves (are thrown into?), and so it is always in the process of being reconstructed: reconstruction is inevitable and everyone is engaged in it all the time; the question is what one's particular actions contribute to it.

I often think of beauty in this context, for two reasons. First, although it is not an "objective" property of things, beauty is not a purely "subjective" feature of the observer either. Because it is not purely subjective, we can argue about it; and because it is not purely objective, we can't ever hope to reach universal agreement about any aesthetic judgment. (If we could, I think, we would be occupying a very sorry world.)

Second, because in finding something beautiful we commit ourselves to wanting to devote ourselves, at least (and at most) partially, to it and to spending part of our life in its presence and company. But in doing so—here I can only assert dogmatically what I try to argue for in *Only a Promise of Happiness*—we are also committed to changing ourselves and, in the process, the beautiful thing, whether a person or an object. The net result is that beauty can stand for the fact that "the world" is a product both of the world that is already there and of our own contribution; it can also allude to the constant change in which reconstruction consists. In addition, since we don't know what will happen to us as a result of our interaction with something we find beautiful, beauty intimates, in addition, the dangers inherent in every effort at reconstruction—dangers we cannot possibly avoid, since, as I just said, reconstruction is inevitable for every one of us.

Costica Bradatan: While there are still important things I would have very much liked to discuss with you, for reasons of space I am afraid we have to draw this conversation to a close. I hope we will have another opportunity to return one day to some of the issues we have covered here, as well as come up with new ones.

It pleases me to say this has been a very illuminating conversation, a fascinating discussion, and I am sure the readers of *The European Legacy* will agree with me on this. It has been for me a great honor and a very enriching experience to moderate it. Simon, Giuseppe, and Alexander: I thank you so much!

★ ★ ★

Hunting Plato's *Agalmata*

∼ Matthew Sharpe ∼

ABSTRACT *In this essay I argue that to understand Plato's philosophy, we must understand why Plato presented this philosophy as dialogues: namely, works of literature. Plato's writing of philosophy corresponds to his understanding of philosophy as a transformative way of life, which must nevertheless present itself politically, to different types of people. As a model, I examine Lacan's famous reading of Plato's Symposium in his seminar of transference love in psychoanalysis. Unlike many other readings, Lacan focuses on Alcibiades' famous description of what caused his desire for Socrates: the supposition that beneath Socrates' Silenus-like language and appearance, there were agalmata, treasures, hidden in his belly. I argue that this image of Socrates can also stand as an image for how we ought to read and to teach Plato's philosophy: as harbouring different levels of insight, couched in Plato's philosophy as literature.*

> *"For Aristophanes I have this suggestion: old, soft, beloved . . . Beloved of whom? In Phaedrus' case, for example, we know by whom—Eryximachus; Agathon, by Pausanias. Aristophanes, I suggest, and this is a mere suggestion, by Plato. There is an old story that when Plato died he had Aristophanes' comedies under his pillow."*
>
> —Leo Strauss, *On Plato's 'Symposium'*

ON THE LITERARY AND PHILOSOPHICAL SIGNIFICANCE OF ARISTOPHANES' HICCUPS

Two facts concerning controversial psychoanalyst Jacques Lacan's eighth seminar on transference, wherein Plato's *Symposium* occupies half the year,[1] might excite hagiographers of twentieth-century ideas. The first is that the seminar was given at nearly exactly the same time as the equally controversial classicist Leo Strauss's famous seminar (Autumn term of 1959) on the dialogue at the University of Chicago. The second is that,

∼

25

at a decisive point, Lacan tells us that—out of his *Eros* for his audience—he has solicited interpretive advice from Strauss's long-time correspondent (and Lacan's teacher) Alexandre Kojeve. Kojeve is an unreformable snob, Lacan comments wryly. And he had not recently revisited the *Symposium*. But Kojeve did deign to tell his younger acolyte this higher exegetical mystery: that you can get nowhere near the true teaching of the *Symposium* if you do not understand why Aristophanes, just as he is about to speak, gets the hiccups (Lacan, IV 11).

Kojeve's sage intervention here concerning Plato's *Symposium* puts on stage directly the literary nature of the Platonic dialogues. Why did Plato, the philosopher whom students everywhere are taught wanted to "expel the poets" from his ideal city, nevertheless present his work in dramatic dialogues, including the kind of sub-philosophical, "literary" interruption which Aristophanes' intergestion in the *Symposium* surely typifies? Why indeed, in these dialogues, did Plato himself violate nearly every proscription he has his Socrates try to put on the imitative poets in the *Republic*, not least the prohibition against speaking indirectly, through characters or mouthpieces? (*Rep.* 392b–398a).

In recent European thought, led by the later work of Michel Foucault (and behind him, Pierre Hadot), there has been growing recognition that classical philosophy—as opposed to its modern successors, analytic and Continental—represented a *bios* or way of life. Far from an impersonal *mathesis*, the learnings and teachings of the philosophers were meant to engender what Plato calls in the *Politeia* a *periagoge tes psuches*, or turning around of the soul, of the initiate (*Rep.* 518c–d). However, certainly in Foucault's published work in the area, what could be called the "literary question" concerning why Plato for one, and Aristotle, might have written dialogues, is not taken up.[2] At least, it is not robustly linked to this recovery of the sense of classical philosophy as *bios theoretikos*.

This essay aims by contrast to address this lack in what is otherwise a welcome return to classical thinking. Its horizon is the hypothesis that Plato's way of writing was deeply connected to his sense of philosophy as a *bios* animated by a particular species of *Eros*. This love or desire for transformative truth singles out would-be philosophers from those who pursue the worldly goods of wealth (the *bios tou pollou*) and/or the political goods of fame (he *bios politikos*). However, Plato's awareness of the different types of human desire legislates a mode of writing which would somehow address all of these different addressees. More than this, the relative openness of the literary, dialoguic form allows Plato to write in different styles (and in different settings) when he addresses the different goods people pursue: so that, for instance, his two great dialogues on *Eros* (*Phaedrus* and *Symposium*) are also his two most rhetorical and poetically compelling compositions. It would follow that when we approach the dialogues unerotically, looking solely for their literal or "purely reasonable" contents, we miss the multiple political, psychological and rhetorical registers that Plato's presentation of his philosophy as literature always involves.

In the modern intellectual division of labour, the one disciplinary field that takes as its object the "Platonic" link between desire or *Eros* and truth is of course psychoanalysis. (This is one reason why it remains so awkwardly situated between the humanities and sciences to this day.) Intriguingly, psychoanalysis is also arguably *the* modern discipline which has made moderns attentive again to the entire rhetorical field we hypothesise to be in play in Plato's literary presentation of his ideas: namely, the ways in which the truth and peoples' desire can be said or "half said" in language, through contradictions, witticisms, puns, metaphors and metonymies, "slips" in the speakers' speeches, and other non-verbal behaviours.

In this light, it is perhaps unsurprising that Lacan was unfazed by his teacher Kojeve's gnomic comment pointing to the literary and philosophical significance of Aristophanes' hiccups in the *Symposium*. Indeed, Lacan takes it in his stride. Lacan goes on to suggest two reasons for this kind of Aristophanic conversion symptom which Plato has seen fit to write into the dramatic fabric of the dialogue. The first is that Aristophanes gets the hiccups during the second speech in the *Symposium*, that of the wealthy pederast Pausanias. People often take this speech to give the "Platonic" account of love between an older teacher and beautiful boys. Yet, Lacan notes, when we read the text in the Greek, we notice that Apollodorus' account ends with this ridiculous, isological (perhaps Isocratic?) punning: *Pausaniou . . . pausomenou*: roughly, "Pausanias paused upon this clause." Then there are sixteen lines on how to stop (*pausesthai*) Aristophanes' hiccups, in which the stem *paus-* is repeated no less than seven times (*Pausaniou . . . pausomenou, pausomai, pausn, pausethai, pausetai*). There is no other instance of such stylised punning elsewhere in Plato. What can it mean, Lacan asks us, if not that "if Aristophanes gets the hiccups it is because during the whole discourse of Pausanius he is convulsed with laughter—and so is Plato!" (IV 12).

In Lacan's reading, Plato's derision towards Pausanias is there to show what a later tradition formulated with the thought that it is nearly impossible for the rich man to enter into the kingdom of heaven: namely, that Pausanias' idea of love as a tidy economic exchange between goods of the body and of the soul misses love's definitively uneconomic preconditions (IV 6–11).[3]

The second reason Lacan highlights to explain Aristophanes' hiccups is that it gives Plato an elegant alibi to shift his speaking position from third, after Pausanias, to fourth out of seven, after the doctor, Eryximachus, has reached his Empedoclean heights. For the question of what an author positions as the central part of his text is a decisive consideration for reading an esoteric text, Lacan notes (VII 10). And, like Leo Strauss and others throughout Western history, Lacan suggests that one component of Plato's philosophical literature is such esotericism, guided by his philosophical sense of the different types and capabilities of his different potential readers:

> Plato in the presentation of . . . his thought had deliberately made a place for enigma, in other words that his thought is not entirely open. [I]n the opinion of all the commentators on Plato, ancient and especially modern . . . an attentive examination of the dialogues shows very evidently that in [them] there is an exoteric and esoteric element, a closed-off element . . . so that those who are not supposed to understand do not understand. This is really structuring, fundamental to everything that has remained to us from Plato's texts. (XII 2)[4]

The "merely literary" matter of the comic poet Aristophanes' hiccups in this way can stand at the outer portico of our attempt here to read Lacan's interpretation of the *Symposium*. In particular, for Lacan it points towards the literally central importance in Plato of Aristophanes' famous account of love or *Eros* as the search for each of our lost "other halves," which Socrates' speech however explicitly rebuts (*Symp.* 205e). Aristophanes' account of love is the only one of the first six, considered speeches on *Eros* which speaks to the disconcerting urgency or what it is like to *be* in love,

Lacan notes.[5] Moreover, these hiccups, which alert us that he is now to take the central spot, anticipate a second major "interruption" in the orderly speaking arrangements of the banqueters in Plato's *Symposium*. This moment also involves Aristophanes. It occurs when the drunken Athenian general and tyrant Alcibiades incongruously bursts in, thereby literally interrupting Aristophanes as he is beginning to object to Socrates' famous *encomium* to the ladder of *Eros* (*Symp.* 212c). Again, any approach inclined to reject such merely literary "curios" is left in the hermeneutically difficult situation of having to ignore, or perhaps even excise,[6] all that follows: namely, Alcibiades' famous *epainos* to Socrates, and account of their torrid, ultimately physically and philosophically unconsummated affair. By contrast, if Aristophanes' attempt to rebut Socrates is interrupted by the drunken entry of Alcibiades, Lacan's reading of Platonic philosophy as literature suggests that this is because Alcibiades is about to show, *in actu*, the abiding force of the comedian's earlier account of love and its passion. Indeed, in what Lacan immodestly suggests might represent "an epoch" in interpreting the *Symposium*, he argues that "the very scenario of what happens between Alcibiades and Socrates [involves] the last word of what Plato has to tell us concerning the nature of *Eros*" (XII 2), hidden behind the scandalous appearance of this encounter.

The central pivot of Lacan's reading, famously, is Alcibiades' description of Socrates as like a satyr whose ugly exterior conceals treasures or *agalmata* which pique Alcibiades' desire, and turn him into Socrates' lover (*erastes*). For Lacan's purposes in the seminars—of trying to put psychoanalytic practice on an adequate theoretical footing—this image of the *agalmata* comes to form the basis for his decisive later notion of the *objet petit a*, cause of desire. For our purposes, by reading Lacan's reading of the *Symposium*, I am going to argue here that Alcibiades' account of what erotically drew him to Socrates can also stand as a guide for how we should interpret classical philosophy in general, and the Platonic dialogues in particular.

DIOTIMA'S ASCENT, SOCRATES' IRONY

So what further evidence does Lacan provide for this ironic Plato? If Aristophanes' speech gives us the element of *Penia* or lack in *Eros*, are not the two succeeding speeches of Agathon and Socrates or Diotima there to fill this lack, and restore to love its other, *Poros* half (203b–e)? And doesn't this element of *Poros* find its most perfect description at the height of Socrates' speech, wherein Diotima evokes the "ocean of Beauty (*kalos*)" upon which the philosophical lover can come finally to gaze, and which by rigid designation, can lack *nothing* (211a–b)?

Lacan's wager is that if we read the text closely, we will see that both Agathon's and Socrates' speech have a "derisory" register which calls into question the dialogue's exoteric surface.

Agathon's speech, the fifth, is for a tragedian the most extraordinarily rococo performance.[7] Love for Agathon is, remarkably, the source and reconciliation of all the virtues, ranging from justice ("for violence never touches love" [196b–c], nor apparently, the police) through to moderation, since we all can agree on how truly moderate lovers are, even in times of disagreement. *Eros* is also most gentle, Agathon sophisticates.

Why? Comparing him to *ate* in Homer, namely the tragic misfortune that befalls people like Oedipus or Antigone, we learn that he only ever walks upon the skulls of men (195d)![8]

Next to this "lovely proof" (195e), we should not be surprised when Agathon's speech climaxes by saying that love brings "*eirenen pen en anthrophois... pereagai de gelanen.*" The idea that love brings "peace (*eirenen*) among men" might strike us as odd coming from a Greek poet in the Homeric line beginning with the *Illiad*. But, Lacan notes, *peleagei de galanin*:

> means absolutely 'nothing is working, dead calm on the deep.' In other words, you have to remember what dead calm on the sea meant for the ancients. That meant: nothing is working any more, the vessels remain blocked at Aulis and, when that happens to you in mid-ocean, it is very embarrassing, just as embarrassing as when that happens to you in bed. So that when one evokes [this] *peleagei de galanin* in connection with love, it is quite clear that you are having a little giggle. (VII 11–12)

So much for Agathon. Our remaining questions to Lacan concern Socrates. Does not Socrates, by gracefully positioning his young self as the proponent of the same position as Agathon's, not proceed to ruthlessly (if a little sophistically[9]) demolish Agathon's position? It turns out that Diotima teaches that *Eros* is neither beautiful nor a God, but our desire to possess some good we lack, supposing only—as the young Socrates lovingly grants his Priestess—"that someone changes the question... and puts 'good' (*agathos*) in place of beautiful (*kalos*)" (204e [sic.]). *Eros* is a *daimon* or spirit that mediates between (*metaxu*) mortals and Gods. Moreover, since we desire to possess what we love for as long as possible, Socrates' or Diotima's conclusion is that *Eros* is the one desire in mortal creatures that naturally aims at what is immortal. This is evident even in the physical *Eros* of beasts and non-philosophers, whose couplings give birth to offspring who outlive their progenitors. So *Eros* immortally becomes under Diotima's guidance the desire to give birth, in beauty, to the most lasting Goods (206b–d). In this manner, as Lacan notes, Socrates' great speech slides from treating beauty as what we might call the handmaiden or midwife of *Eros* towards being its highest object: so it finally becomes "the reason for all [the lover's earlier labours]" (211a). The slide occurs upon the famous "ladder of love" wherein the acolyte passes from loving the beauty of one body, to the beauty in all bodies, then to the beauty in souls, laws and works of culture, before arriving at the idea of Beauty herself (207c–208b; 211b–c) (Lacan, IX 4).

There are at least four reasons why Lacan thinks Aristophanes is right when, at the end of this ascent, he tries to interrupt the group's applause saying, "all the same...," except that Alcibiades' comic entrance stops him short (212c). The first reason is simply Socrates' refusal to avow the doctrine of love as his own, by putting it in the mouth of the Priestess Diotima. This disavowal seems all the more remarkable since Socrates has just restated that *Eros* is the one thing about which he can speak from wisdom (198d). As Lacan put it ironically to his own audience in *Seminar VIII*:

> Suppose that I had to develop all my teachings concerning psychoanalysis... and that—verbally or in writing—in doing it, at a certain moment, I hand over to Francoise Dalto. You would say: 'all the same, why? Why is he doing that?' (VIII 8)

Well, Lacan secondly notes that Diotima herself tells us that the status of her discourse is not something that will match the logical rigour to which Socrates aspires in the *elenchus*, whose paradigm for Plato remained mathematics. Appropriately enough, given her teaching of *Eros* as *metaxu* between mortals and gods, she rather specifies that what she will say is neither *episteme* (knowledge) nor *amathia* (ignorance), but something between (*metaxu*) the two: "It's judging things correctly without being able to give a *logos* . . . correct *doxa* has this character: it is between understanding and ignorance" (202a) (Lacan, VIII 8–9).[10]

Socrates' handing over to Diotima, Lacan can thus correctly emphasise, corresponds to his beginning an approach to the topic of love which transcends what can be achieved through the purely philosophical methods of *elenchus* and *diaeresis*. "In the absence of experimental conquests," Lacan comments, "it is clear that in many domains . . . there will be a pressure to let myth speak":

> What is remarkable is precisely . . . that Plato always knows perfectly well what he is doing or what he makes Socrates do . . . in the realm of myth . . . and throughout the whole Platonic work we see in the *Phaedo*, in the *Timaeus*, in the *Politeia*, myths emerging, when they are required, [namely] to supply for the gap in what can be assured dialectically. (VIII 9)

Thirdly, Lacan draws our attention to the way Diotima's progressively hortatory discourse on the ascent of *Eros* is riddled with inconsistencies only covered by the young Socrates' loving eagerness to agree with everything she has to teach. "What is more," Lacan observes:

> Socrates punctuates these gaps [in Diotima's account] by a whole series of replies which . . . — it is tangible . . . — are more and more bemused. I mean that there are first of all respectful replies of the style: 'do you really think that?', then afterwards: 'very well, let us go as far as you are leading me' and then, at the end, that becomes clearly: 'have fun, my girl, I'm listening, talk away!' (VIII 9)[11]

It is remarkable, given this very bold Lacanian reversal of the accepted reading of the *Symposium* on Diotima, that even his best expositors have not highlighted this decisive prequel to the importance he assigns to Plato's Alcibiades.[12]

Alcibiades and Socrates' *Agalmata*

Lacan argues we should listen when Socrates comments at *Symposium* 208c that really Diotima was speaking "in the manner of a perfect sophist." The culminating reason Lacan gives for such a scepticism towards the apparent "Platonic" teaching on *Eros* in Socrates' speech is the episode that follows it. Alcibiades' performance in his famous *epainos* about Socrates, Lacan comments, has something of the scandalous force that in the older poets characterised the interventions of Gods, when they are moved by *Eros* to cavort with mortals (XI 11–12). Yet our enjoyment of the comedy should not conceal the seriousness of what Alcibiades has to say concerning *Eros*, by recounting his real love for the particular individual, Socrates. We should take note, Lacan argues, that Plato has

Alcibiades seat himself exactly *metaxu* Socrates and Agathon. It is as if Alcibiades is about to *embody* the *metaxu* status of *Eros* we have just theoretically encountered:

> namely, . . . precisely . . . the point we are at, . . . in which the debate is in the balance between . . . the one who knows, and knowing, shows that he must speak without knowing [Socrates] and the one who, not knowing [Agathon], spoke of course like a bird-brain but who nevertheless . . . 'said some very beautiful things' [as Socrates complements Agathon]. (IX 9)

However that may be, Martha Nussbaum concurs that Alcibiades' intervention introduces (in Lacan's words):

> a change of perspective and we must carefully set up the world into which, all of a sudden, after this fascinating mirage, all of a sudden [Alcibiades] replunges us. I say 'replunges' because this world is not the world beyond, . . . it is the world as it is where, after all, we know how love is lived out and that, however fascinating all these beautiful stories appear, an uproar, a shout, a hiccup, the entry of a drunken man is enough to bring us back to [Eros] as it really is. (IX 9)[13]

All the comic aspects of love—comic when it is not we who are involved—are evoked in Alcibiades' account: down to cooked-up attempts to invite Socrates over to dinner and then keep him talking so late that he has no option but to stay over at Alcibiades' for the night (217a–d). Things culminate—after Alcibiades has told the uninitiated to block our ears (218b) (XI 4)—with this momentous exchange beneath the covers on Alcibiades' couch: "You asleep, Socrates?" "No, not at all!" (218c).

Lacan's reading of Alcibiades' confession singles out something other readings generally pass over. It is the central image Alcibiades returns to three times, "in a quasi-repetitive insistence," as he strives to articulate what he immortally dubs Socrates' incomparable *atopia* (XI 3). Alcibiades envisions Socrates as the statuettes "that it seems really existed at the time," whose exteriors were shaped in the likeness of the satyr Silenus (III 2). But this ugly exterior concealed in their insides what Alcibiades calls *agalmata theiōn* ("images of the gods," 215b), *agalmata theia kai thaumasta* ("images divine and wondrous," 216e), and finally *agalmata arêtes* (literally "images of virtue," 222a): in Lacan's gloss, "the marvel of marvels" (XI 3).

Lacan's interest in this striking image of the *agalmata* Alcibiades discerns in Socrates reflects the import which Alcibiades himself assigns to it in his *epainos*. He tells us directly that it was only when he had "opened" Socrates and caught a glimpse of these *agalmata* that his passion was born:

> It was all so golden and all beautiful that there was only one thing to do, *en brachei*, as soon as possible, by the quickest means, to do whatever Socrates commands. (217a)

So "it is not beauty, nor ascesis, nor the identification to God that Alcibiades desires, but this unique object which he saw in Socrates," Lacan observes (XI 10). Indeed, in this privileged object, Lacan is going to argue that Plato has laid out very precisely the coordinates for understanding the key stake in the transferential love psychoanalysts encounter on a daily basis in the clinic (I 11). How is this so?

The word *agalma* in the Greek means roughly "ornament" or "adornment."[14] Nevertheless, as Lacan shows, in the poetry of the Greeks, the signifier *agalma* (nom. pl. *agalmata*) had accrued a set of religious significations which would have been known to Plato's audience as they read the *Symposium*. Perhaps most tellingly, the Trojans' fatal hesitation about what to do with the wooden horse the Greeks had gifted them, recounted in *Odyssey* VIII, concerned whether or not, rather than opening its belly straight away, they should not transport it to the citadel's heights to present it as a *mega agalma*: namely, as a kind of wondrous image to win the *Eros* of the gods.[15]

Just so, Lacan argues, on one side, Alcibiades is very explicit that his *eros* for Socrates is caused because Socrates scorns all the goods of bodily beauty or riches which "the many" are always chasing about, believing that they will deliver *makaria* (happiness) (219d–e). The *agalmata* Alcibiades sees are sacred. These things can not be compared, or circulated amongst other, more profane goods. So there is this truth in Alcibiades' imperative *episthesthe* (bar or close!) "*pulas panu megalas*" ("the heaviest gates") so the uninitiated may not hear what he has to say at 218b, complete with the evocation of the Egyptian mysteries ("*tois usin*").[16]

Yet, at the same time, the transcendent *agalmata* Alcibiades espies in Socrates are clearly tied to the dimension of what Lacan calls a "unique covetousness" proper to *Eros*, completely abstracted from in Diotima's "fascinating mirage" of *Eros* (IX 4).[17]

Agalma is also etymologically related to *agamai*, which means "to admire," but shades off towards "to envy" or "to be jealous of" (X 6). Thus, when Alcibiades tells the assembled of the marvels he has glimpsed in Socrates, it is to stress Socrates' unique, irreplaceable singularity: the very type of irreplaceability which would forestall any Diotimian ascent towards higher, but also more general, truths.[18] Lacan notes how Alcibiades goes to some pains, having invoked Socrates' hidden treasures, to boast that he "doubts whether anyone else has ever been able to see what he is talking about . . . 'no one has ever seen what is in question, as I once happened to see; and I saw it!'" (X 4, paraphrasing *Sym*. 217a). We are dealing, in short, with what Lacan calls "the discourse of passion at its most quaking point" (X 4). In this way, Plato shows himself wide awake to how: "in the action of love, there is introduced this object, precisely from which one [always] wants to ward off competition, an object that one does not even wish to show" to any others (IX 10).[19]

So we have seen two dimensions of the object-cause of Alcibiades' desire, which Lacan highlights. These are: (1) its transcendence vis-à-vis all mundane goods, which situates it in the orbit of sacred Things; and (2) the covetousness its splendour invokes in the *erastes*. There is however a third, epistemic dimension which for Lacan allows us to say that Plato has put "every possible key" before us, in order to understand the nature of *Eros* as it manifests itself in life and in the clinic (I 11).

Near the end of the *encomium*, Alcibiades comments that it is not only Socrates' body that is ugly and Silenus-like but that his words too at first sight seem ridiculous. As other dialogues confirm, Socrates is always banging on about the *technites*—doctors, craftspeople, physical trainers and ship's captains (221e)—and concerns far beneath the aristocratic concerns of the assembled host. Yet Alcibiades likens the effect Socrates' words have on him, despite this rough exterior, to the ecstasy of Cybeline revellers. It is something completely beyond what any other orator—even Pericles—can produce (215d–216b). In a way which again invokes the dimension of the mysteries, Alcibiades confesses that Socrates alone is the one person that can make him feel *aidos* or shame: "you didn't think I had it in me, did you gentleman?" (216a–b). Socrates' discourse even makes him ask whether his life—"*my life*," as Alcibiades underscores—"was no better than a miserable slave's" (215e). So he is torn between love and wanting to flee Socrates, wishing him dead (216c).

The point is that Alcibiades' desire is caused not simply because Socrates has, for him, beautiful *agalmata* in his belly. He testifies that the splendour of these images intimate to him some body of knowledge which he imagines speaks to his most intimate concerns. In so far as he loves Socrates, Socrates is for him the *subjet suppose savoir*: he who has this transformative knowledge at his disposal, if only he can elicit it from him:

> What I thought at that time was that what he really wanted was *me* and that seemed to me the luckiest coincidence: all I had to do was to let him have my way with me and he would teach me everything he knew—believe me, I had a lot of confidence in my sex appeal (*hora*). (217a)[20]

This brings us, to conclude, to what Lacan sees in Socrates' response to this proposition, so shamelessly confessed to the banqueters. Here Lacan's reading notably parts company with Nussbaum' interpretation in *The Fragility of Goodness*. For Nussbaum, Socrates neither knows nor cares to know anything of Alcibiades' truths and way of loving.[21] By contrast, for Lacan, we need to take Socrates' avowal of knowledge concerning *Eros* at *Symposium* 198d seriously. For "it is because he knows" about *Eros*, Lacan contends, that Socrates' response to Alcibiades' transferential crush speaks so directly to the task of the psychoanalyst, confronted with the demands of the analysand (XI 6). What is Lacan's analysis here?

Well, after crudely establishing that Socrates was wide awake beside him as they lay together on Alcibiades' couch, Alcibiades seizes his moment. He confesses that of all his many admirers, Socrates alone seems worthy of his love (218c). This, in short, is the moment when what Lacan calls the "miraculous" dimension of love could have been achieved. This "miraculous" dimension involves the phenomenon which Phaedrus' opening speech in the *Symposium* told us is most beloved of the gods. It occurs when a beloved (*eronomos*), like Achilles in the *Illiad*, returns the love of his or her lover (*erastes*), in this case the older Patroclus (IV 4). It is at this moment that love, in its reciprocal, substitutive dimension, supplants desire, which we all know can remain a one-way street.[22]

Plato dramatises for us in *Alcibiades Major* a fact widely attested: that Socrates was Alcibiades' first lover or desirer. Alcibiades' speech in the *Symposium* however amply attests that since then Alcibiades has become the *erastes* of Socrates: and this in typical Alkibiadean disregard of the scandal which attended a young man actively pursuing an elder.[23]

Socrates, however, famously refuses Alcibiades. Lacan's translates Socrates' wonderful reply to Alcibiades' "proposition" at *Symposium* 219a–b in these terms:

> Really, my dearest Alcibiades, you are really and truly no bad hand at a bargain, if what you say is really true and you see in me some power which can make you better; you must see some inconceivable beauty in me. If then you spy it there and if you are trying to do a deal of beauty for beauty, so instead of the physical appearance of beauty you want to exchange the truth, that would mean nothing other than exchanging bronze for gold. But! Don't be deceiving yourself, examine things more carefully

(*ameinon skopei*) so as not to deceive yourself, and you will see that I properly speaking am nothing (*kenosis*). For the eye of the mind begins to see more sharply when the sight of the eye is losing its keenness, and you are far from that still. (219a–b) (XI 5)[24]

In Lacan's view, it is this austerity in the face of the transferential love of Alcibiades, this attitude of *noli me tangere* (XI 8) that makes of Socrates the ancient prototype of the modern psychoanalyst. The analyst must also enact such an erotic refusal if the transference is not to abort the analysis:

> It is precisely because Socrates knows that he sets his face against having been in any justified or justifiable way whatsoever *eromenos*, the desirable, what is worthy of being loved. (XI 6)

Socrates' very refusal to acknowledge what Alcibiades' *Eros* imagines in Socrates is instead there to turn Alcibiades' erotic gaze around, if the young *erastes* is willing and able to achieve such reflexivity. By not ceding to Alcibiades' transferential supposition, that is, Socrates prompts his *erastes* to consider a type of thing that has clearly never occurred to Alcibiades before: namely, that *if he is so able to "see" such wondrous things in Socrates and others, what must that say concerning the state of his own Eros and psyche*? In other words, it is the refusal of the Socratic physician of the soul that "implicates" Alcibiades on the path towards his own good, *ho agathos*, which for Socrates can only pass by way of *gnothi seauton* (knowledge of the self) (XI 8).

What Socrates gives to Alcibiades, in exchange for his profession of love in the story Alcibiades recounts, is merely the promise that, tomorrow, they should consider what seems best for them both (219b). This is hardly the type of good Alcibiades was after. And in response to Alcibiades' feminine confession to the assembled banqueters in which these mysteries are unclothed, Socrates once again confounds Alcibiades by giving to his words what Lacan calls an "interpretation." The entire, hysterical "satyr play" of unrequited love for Socrates, which Alcibiades has put on stage before us, Socrates interprets, was not so artless as it seemed.[25] It was all produced with an eye to pleasing the most beautiful individual present, to wit, the host so "Platonically" named *Agathon*: [26]

> You're perfectly sober after all Alcibiades. Otherwise you could never have concealed your motive so gracefully. . . . As if the real point of all this has not been simply to make trouble between Agathon and I. You think that I should be in love with you and no one else while you, and no one else, should be in love with Agathon. (222c–d)

Concluding Remarks: From Socrates' to Plato's *Agalmata*

We have now presented what I take to be the key interpretive observations in Lacan's remarkable reading of Plato's *Symposium*. In doing so, we have been newly attentive to several moments of this interpretation passed over, even in the best of the literature on Lacan's impassioned encounter with Plato's *Symposium*.[27]

This erotic encounter has a key place in the history of Lacan's own development. Lacan also boasts the controversial novelty of his reading of Plato's *Symposium* in the much longer history of the ongoing reception of Plato, and what he calls the "longest transference the history of thought has known" (I 4): readers' continuing Alcibiadean attempts to comprehend Socrates' *atopia*.

However, it is pre-eminently as an exemplar of a way of reading the Platonic dialogues that Lacan's reading of the *Symposium* has been proffered here. This way of reading the dialogues starts from an openness to the founding parameters of Plato's thought, lost with the modern, post-Cartesian refiguring of philosophy. It accepts the dimension of philosophy as an erotic pursuit and way of life, whose highest end is the (re-)education of the desire of the philosopher. Our argument is that the formal correlative of this erotic substance of philosophy is, in Plato's case, the dialogic or literary form.

We have seen how Lacan's reading, because it is attuned to the textual elements of setting, action, and interruption in the *Symposium*, presents an interpretation of "Platonic love" strikingly different from the way the *Symposium* is usually understood. The *hyperporos* or over-full speeches of Agathon and Socrates, Lacan suggests, are intended ironically by Plato. If we want to understand Plato's more comprehensive teaching concerning *Eros*, Lacan highlights the fractious encounter that occurs in place of what Aristophanes was clearly about to say in criticism of Socrates' elevated account, when Alcibiades crashes into the room.

That Alcibiades appears like a maddened "satyr" and that his comical acting out is compared by Socrates to a satyr-play—all this, if Lacan is right, is as the fascinating exterior there to capture readers. The scandal conceals the more subtle importance of what Alcibiades' testimony teaches concerning *Eros*. This teaching concerns the place of the erotic—sublime, unattainable objects, *agalmata*—that Alcibiades sees in Socrates' belly. Lacan's argument is that these *agalmata* give poetic figure to the illusory, "transferential" cause of desire analysts must still train themselves to recognise in the desire of their analysands—so they can Socratically renounce it there, thus urging their analysands towards self-knowledge.

The bolder point of this essay though is to make a different extrapolation. This involves saying that Alcibiades' picturing of Socrates as a satyr concealing *agalmata* within, which Lacan highlights, can also stand as a powerful image for how we should read the Platonic corpus itself. If classical philosophy is not to continue to decline—even as both the modern, analytic and Continental streams seemingly approach differing *aporiai*—reviving such an "Alcibidean," or more truly "Socratic," sense of the classical texts in students will be an important part of our philosophic pedagogy.

As I hope also to have indicated, Plato's dialogues amply reward this erotic supposition by, ultimately, prompting us to examine ourselves.

NOTES

1. The key text I refer to in this paper is Jacques Lacan, *Seminar VIII: On Transference*, trans. Cornac Gallagher (London: Karnac Books, 1998). References, including parenthetical references in the text, are to the session (in capitalised Roman numerals), and then the page number. Some translations have been amended by the author.
2. The central work is Michel Foucault, *The History of Sexuality, Volume II, The Use of Pleasure* (London: Penguin, 1992).

3. See Dominic Chiesa, "Le Ressort de L'Amour: Lacan's Theory of Love in His Reading of Plato's *Symposium*," *Angelaki* 2.3 (December 2006): 63. The author is much indebted to this article. Note that a second reason why it seems to me that Aristophanes gets the hiccups, which last throughout the speech of the doctor, Eryximachus, is to highlight the partiality of this technician's proto-scientific account of *Eros* as a physical force of attraction which applies to everything in nature, and which aims to harmonise opposites. Medicine, in this unlikely perspective, becomes *the* erotic art: in Eryximachus' definition, *episteme tou ton somatos erotikwn* (the science of the body's loves) *pros pklesmonen kai kenosis* (for filling and emptying), and restoring the body's physical *harmonia*. But while the good doctor is dryly holding forth thus in justification of his *techne*, Aristophanes is there in the background sneezing unharmoniously, holding his breath, before finally using a feather to tickle his nose!
4. See Lacan, VI 7.
5. See also Lacan, VII 13–15. As such, Aristophanes is the first to say something which we moderns recognise about the phenomenon, conditioned as we are culturally by modern romantic notions of love. By contrast, as Lacan had addressed three years prior, for the ancients love was an essentially comic phenomenon. The play of masks, misidentifications, and metamorphoses in Ovid is as much witness to this as Aristophanes' plays. Equally, it is no mistake that Plato makes his Aristophanes alone the one to make the true point that, if we are to talk comprehensively of *Eros*, the delicate matter of the gods' artful placement and shaping of our genitals should be raised (Lacan, VI 16). See Jacques Lacan, *Seminar V: The Formations of the Unconscious* trans. Cormac Gallagher (London: Karnac Books, 1998), VII, 13–17.
6. Lacan cites the example of the medieval Louis le Roy, who *did* excise this part of *Symposium* from his translation (II 6).
7. Things get so bad that Agathon invokes the image of this youngest of the gods (for love loves the young, 195a–b) prancing around with flowers in his hands, in a way which might evoke for today's readers a commercial for a toilet deodorant: "His place is wherever it is flowery and fragrant; there he settles, there he stays" (196b).
8. For Lacan on *Ate*, a notion to which he devoted some time in the year preceding his work on the *Symposium*, see Jacques Lacan, *Seminar VII: The Ethics of Psychoanalysis*, trans. Dennis Porter, ed. Jacques-Alain Miller (New York: W.W. Norton, 1996), 262–70.
9. And then sophistically eliding the difference between desire and love in the Greek word *Eros*, at 200a–b and 202d.
10. Lacan, IX 6; see Chiesa, "Le Ressort de L'Amour," 66.
11. See also IX 3 and IX 8 for Lacan's further supporting claims.
12. For instance Chiesa, "Le Ressort de L'Amour," 66–67; but see also the excellent critical reading of Lacan's *Symposium* in Paul Allen Miller, "Lacan, the *Symposium*, and Transference," in *Postmodern Spiritual Practices: The Construction of the Subject and the Reception of Plato in Lacan, Derrida, and Foucault* (Ohio: Ohio State University Press, 2007), 121–30.
13. Martha Nussbaum, *The Fragility of Goodness: Luck and Ethics in Greek Tragedy and Philosophy* (Cambridge: Cambridge University Press, 2001).
14. Notably enough in our context, Lacan notes the semantic proximity of *agalma* to *agastos*, "the admirable," from which Plato himself derives *agathon* in the etymological follies in *Cratylus* (Lacan, X 7).
15. See Lacan, X 7–8. Lacan cites several other cases. The golden ornaments crafted to adorn the horns of the heifers Telemachus sacrifices to Athena in the *Odyssey* III, for instance, are *agalmata*. We are told that they pleased the eye or gratified (*kecharoizen*) the goddess (X 7). In Euripides' *Hecuba*, the tree at the sacred site of Delos under which Leta is supposed to have given birth to Apollo is *odinos agalma dias*: a standing *agalma* of the birth-pains of the goddess (X 5).
16. See also *Symp.* 220c on Socrates' character.
17. NB: Every bit as much as it was lost in the technical discourse of Eryximachus before Aristophanes' speech. Prompted by Lacan's analysis, it is tempting to see the *Symposium*'s ordered speeches as divided into two halves of three speeches. At the end of both halves,

we have ascended out from the pressing bodily dimension of *eros*, to which Aristophanes the comedian is there to return us.

18. See Nussbaum, *The Fragility of Goodness*, 185–87.
19. See *Symp.* 214d.
20. This is exactly the type of erotic-economic exchange that Plato has introduced in the speech of Pausanias, which Lacan argues Plato has artfully shown his criticism of.
21. Nussbaum, *The Fragility of Goodness*, 165, 189–90. This is what is in play for Nussbaum when Alcibiades asks Socrates rhetorically whether Socrates will "let him" tell the truth.
22. When love happens, Lacan concurs with Phaedrus in his own "Platonic" *mythos* of sorts, it is as if you had reached out to grasp a flower on a branch, and that—because of your reaching— it suddenly burst into bloom. And then, miracle of miracles, a hand reaches back from the bloom to clasp yours (IV 3).
23. See Nussbaum, *The Fragility of Goodness*, 188 on this point; see also Miller, "Lacan, the *Symposium*, and Transference," 125–27.
24. On Socrates' "nothingness" or *kenosis*, see Lacan, XI 5–6, and *Symp.* 175d.
25. In the Greek theatre, the comedy and tragedy were followed by a satyr play. Aristophanes has given us our comedy and Agathon has spoken as a tragedian. So we might be tempted to read the banquet here, as a "real" Dionysian festival wherein the truly highest artist, Socrates, can be awarded the prize.
26. On the Platonic play in this name, see, amongst others, Miller, "Lacan, the *Symposium*, and Transference," 124–25.
27. Neither Chiesa nor Miller, for instance, stresses the decisive importance of Aristophanes' hiccups for Lacan, in placing Aristophanes as the central speaker, although they both make many other fine interpretations. No previous reader, as far as this author is aware, has located how ironic Lacan takes Socrates' Diotimian account of love to be. However, this seems decisive if his reading of Alcibiades' importance is to be plausible.

The Nexus of Unity of an Emerson Sentence

∼ KELLY DEAN JOLLEY ∼

ABSTRACT *In this essay I investigate the unity of Emerson's sentences. I begin by describing the phenomenology of reading Emerson and use that phenomenology to orient the investigation. I propose to understand the unity of Emerson's sentences by using a variation of Frege's strategy for understanding the unity of sentences generally. I then address how the unity of the Emerson sentence serves to create the unity of the Emerson paragraph and even of the Emerson essay. Along the way I compare Emerson's essays to Lancelot Andrewes' sermons. I finish by using the results of the investigation and comparisons to provide a partial reading of ''Experience'' in which I shed light on the nature of Emerson's encounter with the problematic of skepticism.*

> *To undergo an experience with something—be it a thing, a person, or a god —means that this something befalls us, strikes us, comes over us, overwhelms and transforms us. When we talk of ''undergoing'' an experience, we mean specifically that the experience is not of our own making; to undergo here means that we endure it, suffer it, receive it as it strikes us and submit to it. It is this something itself that comes about, comes to pass, happens.*
>
> *To undergo an experience with language, then, means to let ourselves be properly concerned by the claims of language by entering into it and submitting to it. If it is true that man finds the proper abode of his existence in language—whether he is aware of it or not—then an experience we undergo with language will touch the innermost nexus of our existence. We who speak the language may thereupon become transformed by such experiences, from one day to the next or in the course of time.*
>
> —Martin Heidegger, ''The Nature of Language''[1]

GETTING STARTED

The phenomenology of reading Emerson is easiest to capture if we consider the serious virgin reader of Emerson. Such a reader finds the sentences of an Emerson essay a string of pearls loosely strung.[2] Emerson sentences seem pearly, lustrous, and the sentences seem self-contained, even self-centered, wholes—hard and indivisible. The sentences seem as though they could be rearranged without injury to any one. Each sentence's nexus of unity appears epigrammatic.

∼

Worse, as the reader attends more closely to an Emerson sentence, it seems *merely* epigrammatic, in one of two ways—as a coarse thought in finely turned words, a day laborer in genteel get-up; or as all surface, incorporeal. The second way most interests me. It is common and commonly frustrating to the serious virgin reader. This aspect of the phenomenology of reading an Emerson sentence is one of which Emerson himself supplies a fine description: "I cannot get it nearer to me . . . I take this evanescence and lubricity of all objects, which lets them slip through our fingers when we clutch hardest, to be the most unhandsome part of our condition."[3] An Emerson sentence seems evanescent and lubricated, slippery. When the reader tries to take hold of one, it slips through his fingers.

Even worse, an Emerson sentence seems to be unconnected with other Emerson sentences. There are no inter-sentential connections (logical or discursive) that allow the reader to break the sentence's surface. It's as though the sentence's form so controls the sentence that it attenuates the sentence's content. Content attenuated, nothing bodies out the sentence.

Even worse still, despite the form's control of individual sentences, it seems no form controls Emerson's writing above the level of the individual sentence. The content of any essay, such as it is, seems somehow to be the forms of the individual, bodiless sentences. The reader cannot get the sentences, and so the essay, nearer to him. The individual words of the essay seem to cross-refer in some way, but not to refer. It seems nothing is being talked about.[4]

I am trying to capture an aspect of the serious virgin reader's phenomenology in reading Emerson, but I don't think that only the serious virgin reader experiences this aspect—no, it is a permanent feature of even the serious consummate reader's reading of Emerson. She will find Emerson's prose built in such a way that it must seem superficial, all surface, from time to time, despite her inward sympathetic frequentation of it. As I see things—and I am not trying to dictate terms, but rather accurately to register my sense of the difficulty—Emerson builds his prose according to his particular sense of *ordonnance*, *exactness* and *relevant absorption*. What particular sense is that?

I mentioned the words of an Emerson sentence. I need now to concentrate on them. An Emerson sentence seems as it does to a serious virgin reader because she is rapt by the sentences of an Emerson essay. But the serious consummate reader, in her best moments anyway, is rapt by the words of an Emerson essay.

A LITTLE FREGE, A LITTLE WITTGENSTEIN

I am preparing to investigate what I call *the nexus of unity* of an Emerson sentence. I intend to discipline my investigation by making use of certain notions of Gottlob Frege's.

When Frege described the logic of language, he began by noting that a sentence is a unity.[5] That may seem less than philosophically interesting; it may seem nothing more than a commonplace encountered on the first page—perhaps in the first sentence—of a grammar book. But Frege meant that sentences are unities in a way that outstrips the meaning of a commonplace claim in a grammar book, even when featured on its first page. Frege meant that sentences are unities essentially, and that they have "parts" only when deconstructed, in abstraction. To see why this is philosophically interesting, consider what we would more naively think about sentences: we think of them as being composed word-by-word. When we think this way, we are thinking of the word, and not of the sentence, as the real unit of meaning. Individual words have meanings. In the light of those meanings, we select words, add them together, and build sentences. Sentence-meaning is composed of, is a function of, word-meanings.

But Frege turns this topsy-turvy. Frege thinks of the sentence as the real unit of meaning. Words have meanings only as they occur in sentences. Word-meaning is decomposition of, a function of, sentence-meaning. Frege made of this a rule for thinking, and in particular a rule for philosophical investigation: "Never ask for the meaning of a word except in the context of a [sentence]."[6] I think the rule must be specially kept when reading Emerson.

It may seem I have lost my way. I began by talking about Emerson's reader attending to sentences, and then I suggested that his reader should attend to words. But then I dipped into Frege only to emerge with a rule that directs attention away from words and onto sentences. And I commended the rule to Emerson's reader. What am I up to?

Before trying to answer, I need to extend the Frege I've introduced by looking briefly into Ludwig Wittgenstein's *Tractatus* distinction between signs and symbols.[7] Wittgenstein's distinction rests on Frege's rule.

To understand the distinction, we need an example. Consider the following two sentences.

(a) Albuquerque is a city in New Mexico.
(b) Las Vegas is no Albuquerque.

In (a) and (b) there occurs the same *sign*: 'Albuquerque.' But 'Albuquerque' is not the same *symbol* in (a) and (b). Wittgenstein says that we can only "see the symbol in the sign" if we see the sign "in the context of significant use."[8] This is Wittgenstein's way of quoting Frege's rule. We can only see the symbol in 'Albuquerque' by considering the sign in the context of the sentence, the context of significant use. When we consider sentence (a), we see that in it 'Albuquerque' is used as a proper (place) name. But that is not how it is used in sentence (b). In (b), 'Albuquerque' is used adjectivally. Same sign, different symbols: Wittgenstein thinks this one-many relationship occurs constantly in philosophy, much to the confusion, much to the chagrin of philosophers.[9]

When I commend Frege's rule to Emerson's reader, I do so because it is necessary for reading Emerson that his reader see the symbols in his signs. To attend to the words of an Emerson essay requires attending also to his sentences. In other words, rightly attending to Emerson's words is not a task that can be carried out in isolation from attending to his sentences. But the focal point of attention is the words, not the sentences, in a way that I will clarify below. So what am I up to? I am up to this: I am up to finding a way of reading Emerson that will allow us to see what he is up to as he constructs his sentences.

I now need two paired Fregean notions—the notions of the unsaturated and the saturated. Again, for Frege, the real unit of meaning is the sentence. When Frege decomposes a sentence, he does so in a way that carries with it the priority of the sentence to its "parts." Frege decomposes a (simple) sentence into an unsaturated and a saturated "part." The unsaturated "part" carries the frame of the sentence with it. Frege symbolizes this by writing that "part" with a blank spot, with empty parentheses. So, for example,

(c)   Kelly is a father.

Frege decomposes (c) into an unsaturated "part": *( ) is a father*, and into a saturated "part": *Kelly*. In the unitary sentence, the saturated "part" saturates the unsaturated "part." Frege understands the distinction between the unsaturated and saturated as a distinction that can only be drawn in the context of a sentence. To use Wittgenstein's terminology, no word, no sign, on its own is either unsaturated or saturated. To be either is to be such that a symbol can be seen in the sign. And a symbol can only be seen in a sign in the context of significant use, in the context of the sentence. I'll come back to the unsaturated below.

I should add, before I conclude these preliminaries, that I am going to employ the Frege and Wittgenstein I have adduced in a less-than-straightforward way. You might say that I am going to use what I have adduced as a kind of negative analogy. Here's what I mean. Emerson uses language strangely—with a kind of strangeness that it is a central concern of this essay to disclose. The Frege and Wittgenstein I have adduced have not been adduced because I plan to show that Emerson's use of language can be domesticated by notions from Frege and Wittgenstein. But I do think that there is an analogy between what I have adduced from Frege and Wittgenstein, and what Emerson does with language, enough of an analogy for us to be able to say—"See, look at how Frege and Wittgenstein bring into view what Emerson is doing, how it is *like* what they have taught us to see, even while he is *not* doing anything straightforwardly Fregean or Wittgensteinian." This is what I have in mind by a kind of negative analogy.

FIELDS OF CONSCIOUSNESS

The unity of an Emerson essay is embodied in what I will call its elemental words. (To embody the unity is to carry the frame of the sentence.) I am purposefully using Heidegger's term: "[W]e must avoid uninhibited word mysticism. Nevertheless, the ultimate business of philosophy is to preserve the *force of the most elemental words* . . . and to keep common understanding from leveling them off to that unintelligibility which functions in turn as a source of pseudo-problems" (emphasis in the original).[10] I admire Heidegger for his caution about the uninhibited word mysticism that preserving the force of the most elemental words is easily confused with. Unfortunately, I fear that Heidegger does not always take his own caution fully to heart. Emerson, by contrast, almost always does—because he is clearer than Heidegger sometimes is about something crucial, namely that it is not a word as such that is elemental, but rather the occasion of a word. No lexicon of elemental words can be produced ahead of confrontations with the occasions of words. As a result, in isolation from occasions, a word can be neither elemental nor non-elemental. On its occasions, the word will be either one or the other. (I note here that I will sometimes allow myself to telescope the expression, 'the occasion of a word' into 'a word.' But I intend the full phrase across the essay, and I intend to embrace the consequences of the full phrase.) The occasions of the elemental words of an essay light a field of consciousness.[11]

The occasions of other words of the essay mark structural features of the field. Ordonnance, the arrangement and structure of words, occurs in Emerson particularly as it does because of the role of an essay's elemental words. A field of consciousness does not have the arrangement and structure of an argument, nor does it have the arrangement and structure of typical discursive prose. A field of consciousness is a kind of circle: its 'center' is everywhere, its 'circumference' nowhere. Emerson's authorship finds its 'center' in each of Emerson's essays; each of the essays finds its 'center' in each of its individual sentences; and each of the sentences finds its 'center' in the elemental words of the essay. The 'circumference' of each—authorship, essay, sentence, elemental word— is nowhere. The lack of a 'circumference' explains why Emerson essays lack beginnings and endings. An Emerson essay no more has a beginning and an ending than does a painting. I am not denying that each essay starts and finishes.

This is why exactness, specifically exactness in the choice of words, matters so for Emerson. He chooses his elemental words exactly: they are the words whose occasion lights up the field of consciousness explored in the essay. He chooses other words exactly, since they mark structural features of the field, and the field's structure must be correctly mapped. At each occasion of each elemental word, Emerson puts the word under intense pressure, so as to get as much light from it as possible. To the extent that an Emerson essay has an overall structure, it is the structure made of (and made by) its elemental words, not of its paragraphs or sentences. For those who look to paragraphs or sentences for the marks of philosophical progress, Emerson's prose seems to stand still. Yet for those who can look to words for the marks of philosophical progress, Emerson's prose is constantly on the stretch. Emerson's ability to map a field of consciousness is what it is because of his sensitivity to words, to words' behavior in their near and far contexts, to words' congregational ties to other words. As Emerson moves among his words, he makes discoveries about them, and so about the structure of the field of consciousness he is mapping.

This is why relevant absorption occurs particularly as it does in Emerson. As he writes, he becomes absorbed in the field of consciousness he is mapping—he must—and what he does with each individual sentence and with the paragraphs and with the essay is shaped by that absorption. For Emerson, it is not (as Bertrand Russell once said) the verb of a sentence that embodies the unity of the sentence, or not necessarily—it is elemental words. The unity of the sentence, if the sentence works as Emerson wants, is embodied by the elemental words—as is the unity of the paragraph, of the essay, as is the unity of the field of consciousness. It is because the elemental words embody unity that their occasions light up a field of consciousness. (The field of consciousness he is mapping is not his. Emerson is "rendering back to you your consciousness"[12]—but of course it is no more yours than his.)

A Lancelot Andrewes Interlude: Moving Backwards, Moving Forwards

I know I'm moving quickly. I need to brake and supply details. To supply them effectively, I need to unpocket this: Ordonnance, exactness and relevant absorption are features of the prose of Lancelot Andrewes that T. S. Eliot stresses in his essay on Andrewes.[13] I have taken these up deliberately. Emerson's essays and Andrewes' sermons are closely related, and in ways made clear by Eliot. Given this, I can clarify what I am saying by examining briefly Eliot's understanding of ordonnance, exactness and relevant absorption in Andrewes.

When describing Andrewes' prose, Eliot quotes F. E. Brightman:

> But the structure is not merely an external scheme or framework: the internal structure is as close as the external. Andrewes develops an idea he has in mind: every line tells and adds something. He does not expatiate, but moves forward: if he repeats, it is because the repetition has a real force of expression; if he accumulates, each new word or phrase represents a new development, a substantive addition to what he is saying. He assimilates his material and advances by means of it. His quotation is not decoration or irrelevance, but the matter in which he expresses what he wants to say. His single thoughts are no doubt often suggested by the words he borrows, but the thoughts are made his own, and the constructive force, the fire that fuses them, is his own.[14]

What Brightman says of Andrewes is an apt description of Emerson's prose. The structure of an Emerson essay is not merely an external scheme or framework. Anyone who looks for such a structure in an essay will be frustrated. It is the internal structure, an exceptionally close structure, that does the main structuring work. The internal structure is a structure of words, not of sentences, at least not primarily. The elemental words are the forwarding principles of the essay. As they repeat, Emerson finds new force of expression in them. As they accumulate, Emerson adds dimensions to what he is saying. Emerson assimilates what he has read, he brings it to each essay, and he advances by means of it. Advances—that is key: Emerson's incessant quoting is not rightly understood as irrelevant (that should be clear); but it is also not rightly understood as decorative. Emerson's quoting is more disciplined than that. Emerson is thinking through the words of others. In them, he expresses what he wants to say—which, while related to what the others said in them, need not be what they said in them. Emerson makes the words of others his own words; he uses them as he will; he re-fuses the words be borrows.[15] This describes an extraordinary prose—a prose which appears to repeat, to stand still, but is nevertheless proceeding in a particularly deliberate and orderly manner.

Eliot describes Andrewes' prose like this:

> Reading Andrewes ... is like listening to a great Hellenist expounding a text of the *Posterior Analytics*: . . . . dwelling on a single word, comparing its use in its nearer and in its most remote contexts, purifying a disturbed or cryptic lecture-note into lucid profundity. To persons whose minds are habituated to feed on the vague jargon of our time, when we have a vocabulary for everything and exact ideas about nothing ... Andrewes may seem pedantic and verbal. It is only when we have saturated ourselves in his prose, followed the movement of his thought, that we find his examination of words terminating in the ecstasy of assent. Andrewes takes a word and derives the world from it; squeezing and squeezing the word until it yields a full juice of meaning which we should never have supposed any word to possess.

Eliot, like Brightman, provides a description apt of Emerson. Emerson's disciplines of quotation are like the Hellenist's in expounding of a text of the *Posterior Analytics*. By quoting as he does—and not in the way that typical scholarship demands—Emerson is working on and over what he quotes, doing things to it like obsessing over a particular word that the original author may not have used deliberately, moving words from context to context, and purifying what may have been a disturbed or cryptic line into lucid profundity. And Emerson's quotation is not as it were exhausted across the length of a single line; it continues across the length and breadth of the essay. Emerson's prose can seem pedantic and verbal—that is a specification of the superficiality that I was describing as I started this essay. But for the serious consummate reader, Emerson's prose loses its superficiality. When saturated in Emerson's prose, we first see that it builds (elemental) word by (elemental) word, and then we see that Emerson's examination of words can—and often does—terminate (in Eliot's happy phrase) in the ecstasy of assent.

Experiencing Emersonian Unsaturatedness

Emerson's elemental words are unsaturated. The best way to explain what I have in mind is to begin with this: there are varieties of unsaturatedness. Frege carved out a "genus," so to speak, not a "singularity." An Emerson elemental word is unsaturated in that it carries with it not just the frame of the sentence it occurs in, but also the 'frame' of the essay itself. We can symbolize this by varying Frege's empty parentheses—say, by using empty brackets. (I will do so below.) Note here that the negative analogy I spoke of above should be kept in mind. To say that an Emerson elemental word carries with it not just the frame of the sentence it occurs in, but also the 'frame' of the essay itself is not to say that the essay is thus rendered one long, run-on sentence. The way in which the elemental word carries the frame of its sentence is different from the way in which it carries the 'frame' of the essay. Another way of saying this is to say that the elemental word unifies both its own sentence and the essay it appears in, where the two unifications, while alike, differ.

One thing we need to remember: Emerson's elemental words are his, but only after they are ours. What Emerson typically does with his elemental words is first to display them to us in a context (a sentence) in which we will take seeing the symbol in the sign as effortless. We will see the conventional or common symbol in the sign. But then Emerson will recontextualize the word, and the new context will be one in which seeing the conventional symbol in the sign will be problematized. The conventional symbol may, so to speak, hover around the sign—but it is no longer the symbol we see in the sign. Sometimes the etymological symbol will begin to be visible in the sign; sometimes it merely hovers, too, along with the conventional symbol. Emerson recontextualizes until he has what he wants: until we see the symbol he wants us to see in the sign. When that happens, Emerson expects us to recur (whether in fact, by turning pages, or in recollection, by returning our attention) to the beginning of the essay again, and to follow it through, seeing Emerson's symbol in the sign—taking the word as elemental. When we do so, we will see that the elemental word does more than embody the unity of a sentence: it embodies the unity of the essay.[16] Emerson's recontextualizing is one way in which he manages to write on more than one level at once. The reader who never sees anything more than the conventional symbol in the sign will typically not find the essay nonsensical. (The reader I'm imagining here is one who is not yet a serious virgin reader.) Such a reader may even find useful things reading as he does. But he will not have found the philosophical meat of Emerson's writing, but rather only the philosophical milk of it, if that.

Two examples of elemental words are the words 'find' and 'surface' in "Experience."[17] "Experience" is a mapping of the field of consciousness we might term the field of consciousness of undergoing—of having something befall us, come over us, overwhelm and transform us. The short point of the essay is that we are disloyal to what we undergo, to what happens to us. We lose it; we cannot rightly value it. We disrelish enduring, suffering, sufferance. Our disrelish for these leads to an inappetence for our own experience. We will not mind our own business. What Emerson does in the essay is to bring undergoing as a field of consciousness into view: we come to see it and not to see through it—or worse, to refuse it as a field of consciousness. (And it is not merely one field of consciousness among many, but something like the field of consciousness of fields of consciousness—say it is the meta-field of consciousness.[18])

Emerson begins "Experience" by asking "Where do we find ourselves?" He ceremoniously places 'find' midway through a sentence that introduces us as in the middle of a stair in the mid-world. 'Find' carries the frame of the first sentence as well as the frame of the essay. We might symbolize the word in this complicated role: *[( )]find[( )]*. The word matters greatly, embodies the unity of the essay. As Emerson uses it, it is a word at once of receptivity and spontaneity: we find and are found. Think of two of the possibilities of accent in the first sentence: Where do *we find* ourselves? Where do we *find ourselves*? In the first, we are the finders, we do it; in the second, we are found, foundlings, it happens to us. But the dominant note in the word as Emerson uses it is the note of receptivity, not spontaneity. This reversal of dominant notes—we would expect spontaneity to be the dominant note—is an example of Emerson's aversive use of words.[19]

Emerson returns to 'find' twice at the essay's close: (1) About the lords of life: "as I find them in my way." In this sentence, 'find' shows its elemental force. Emerson underscores this by the word's (and phrase's) (at least) tripled extralocutionary force: "as I find them in my way": as obstacles; "as I find them in my way": as objects scattered along the line of my march; "as I find them in my way": as the end-results of my idiosyncratic method of thinking and writing. (2) "But I have not found that much was gained by manipular attempts to realize the world of thought." Here we have the word with spontaneity as the dominate note—but in a sentence in which Emerson is poising himself to reject a certain type of spontaneity, and to embrace receptivity, specifically patience.[20] Emerson embraces patience as a means of self-reclamation, as a means of returning us to loyalty to our experience, as a means of (re-)possessing our souls: "In your patience possess ye your souls" (Luke 21:19).

An empiricist theorizes experience within the problematic of underdetermination: experience is incompetent to tell us what to make of our experience; a supplement of theory is needed. Experience underdetermines what we should believe or may hope or can know. But Emerson shuns theorizing experience within the problematic of underdetermination—although he clearly understands the problematic intimately. (I'll have more to say about this shortly.) What Emerson does is call us back to our experience, and urges us to attend to it more carefully and, especially, more faithfully. What he believes we will recognize is that the problematic of underdetermination grips us only because it baits-and-switches us. The problematic demands that we shape our philosophical imaginations according to its structure: here, on one side, experience (whatever it is); there, on the other side, the world (whatever it is). The problematic then asks us, as it were in a tin, mechanical voice, to "mind the gap." Emerson will have none of this. What he will have is freedom from the problematic and its shaping of our philosophical imagination. He will require that we look again at experience—but not as a 'here' gapped from a 'there,' put into a relation to something else from the start. He will require that we look at experience as the appearing of what there is, of what is real. What is real is as much 'here' as experience itself is—we might say that they occupy 'the same place.' There is no gap to mind. Emerson works within the unproblematic of experience—and that for all his sense of the problems of experience. Emerson knows the problems; but he thinks they are rightly understood only if they are theorized within the unproblematic of experience.

A fascinating and unexpected feature of "Experience," given that the essay is in large part a reworking of the philosophical conception of experience, is that Emerson nowhere invests himself in talk of 'appearances.' His chosen term, instead, is 'surfaces.' By itself, this vocabulary shift is a powerful reworking of a problem of experience. Emerson's "skepticism" is expressed in his anxiety that all he knows of things are their surfaces. Etymologically, 'surface' talks of that face of things that floats, as it were, just above them ('superface' from 'superficies'). Taken this way, the word displaces Kant's talk of 'phenomenon.' Emerson gives us an image of something hidden beneath its surface; Kant gave us a picture of two somethings, one real, the other a resembling bit of papier-mâché, glued together by our categories.[21] The difference may not seem like it makes a difference, but like most changes of a feature of a problem of experience, it does. The anxiety of skepticism is now not about whether we can know a thing at all, but rather whether we can know all of it, can see to the bottom of it. To think of the anxiety of skepticism in this way is to degree our knowledge (how much of a thing do we know?), and to create room for the suggestion that our failure to know more (instead of to know at all) may be as much a matter of what we will not know as of what we cannot know.

At one point in the essay, Emerson appears to advocate a skeptical solution to his reworking of the problem of experience: "We live amid surfaces, and the true art of life is to skate well on them." But Emerson makes this apparent solution difficult to take at face value. He begins the next sentence with 'Under': "Under the mouldiest conventions, a man of native force prospers just as well as in the newest world, and that by skill of handling and treatment. He can take hold anywhere." Since Emerson has earlier expressed the anxiety of (his) skepticism by talking of hands and of unhandsome parts, these sentences make an especially striking sequel to the skating sentence. Notice that taking hold, the polar complement to skating, is not a matter of cognitive achievement ("Life is not intellectual or critical, but sturdy"[22])—it is a matter of native force. The man of native force is poised amid things, and his poise allows him to husband them, take hold of them, and of the moments in which they come to him: the potluck of his day.

A helpful backdrop to Emerson's toiling with skepticism is this: We can think of ourselves as being often attracted to one of two pictures of the self and its experience: On one picture, the self and its experience swells to somehow include all possible objects of knowledge. To come to know on this picture is really just to come to attend. Knowing is modeled on attending to what was previously inattentively noticed. (Plato's theory of recollection is a specification of this picture; Leibniz's monadology is another.) On the other picture, the self and its experience shrinks to an extensionless point, and includes no possible object of knowledge, includes, in fact, very little, almost nothing. To come to know on this picture is really purely passive, inactive. Knowing is like being suddenly rained on. Knowledge is inexpectant spectation. (Hume's epistemology is a specification of this picture; Locke's another.) Despite his emphasis on undergoing, on patience, Emerson is not advocating the picture of the shrunken self-and-experience. I take Emerson to be advocating a picture that combines the two pictures, and that, by so doing, moderates each. Unlike the swollen self-and-experience picture, Emerson recognizes that we live not so much in our bodies as in our non-bodily circumstances. But that recognition does not push Emerson in the direction of the shrunken picture. While we live in our non-bodily circumstances, it is also true that we live in moderately ordered non-bodily circumstances. The shrunken picture makes of our non-bodily circumstances a pure chaos of contingency. Emerson wants to find a way to emphasize *undergoing*, but without embracing the shrunken picture, the spectatorial picture. So what he does is to gad into action the (circumstanced) spectator. When we allow ourselves to fall prey to the shrunken picture, we simply look out on surfaces and we feel we can take hold of nothing. But, when we activate ourselves and are spectators no longer, things change. Surfaces are no longer blinds but are instead handholds. We shift from being eye-minded to being hand-minded. The distinction between appearance and reality is a different distinction for the spectator than it is for the actor: for the spectator, the distinction is, we might say, a logical one—the spectator calculates whether or not what is before him is appearance or reality via judgments about consistency, coherence, simplicity, etc. But for the actor, the distinction is not a logical one, but, let's say, an efficient one—the surfaces of things are not detachable from them or from the entire perceptual fate of the things. For the actor, things further appear instead of disappear in the course of action; and patience is required for the determination of the thing as merely apparent or real, and, if real, as a real somewhat.[23]

Here I need to address another of the essay's elemental words—'illusion.' 'Illusion' is not 'surface': one of the subtle achievements of the essay is the contrast that Emerson insists upon between illusions and surfaces. Unlike the distinction between surfaces and reality, the distinction between illusion and reality is insensitive to the distinction between actor and spectator, or it is at least differently sensitive to it. When we become spectatorial, when the things we are among seem to retreat behind their surfaces, when we seem blinded to them by seeing (only) their surfaces, the trouble is not a projected trouble. It is not that we are gilding and staining our world, but rather that we move from being present among the things that circumstance us to having them present before us. Thus, surfaces. Not thus, illusions.

For Emerson, illusions are a projected trouble. We intermingle ourselves, specifically our imagined and imaginative selves, among things. As I understand Emerson, he thinks of our illusions as resultant from a desire to shift responsibility from us onto things. We want the pleasures and displeasures of being wordlings blamed on the world. We do this for various reasons—but central is our anxiety about recognizing ourselves as contributing authors of our experience. We fear that we cannot or will not recognize what we contribute. *Cannot*—leaving us forever suspicious that our experience is, in part, permanently misunderstood by us; or, *will not*—leaving us forever nettled by the worry that our experience is, in part, disowned by us. We can, however, typically recognize what we contribute, just as we will typically recognize it: but to do so we have to believe in ourselves—which, in Emerson, means that we have to befriend ourselves. To befriend ourselves is to trust ourselves—to think of ourselves as revelators of truth—and to be tender with ourselves. Emerson's essay, "Friendship," manages, among other things, to allegorize the proper relationship of our moods to each other. When Emerson complains famously in "Circles" that "our moods do not believe in each other"[24]—and I do take him to be complaining, not noting, and certainly not noting a necessity—he thinks that the problem's remedy is to be found in our moods befriending one another, in their treating each other tenderly as revelators of the real.

FINAL WORD

I can now say a word more about the apparent contentlessness of Emerson's writing. Emerson's work is *formal*, through and through (at least in one sense of that polytropic term): he is mapping fields of consciousness. In doing so, he is not providing the content of the fields—what they might be, in any given instance, fields of consciousness *of*. The content of an Emerson essay is a field of consciousness. Emerson sees through things to the cradles of things. Emerson's content is form.

NOTES

I thank Stanley Cavell, David O'Conner, James Bell, Russell Goodman, and James Shelley. I wrote the first drafts of this essay in Albuquerque, New Mexico, during the 2005 NEH Summer Seminar on Emerson (directed by Russell Goodman). I thank the NEH for its support.

1. These paragraphs begin Heidegger's long essay, "The Nature of Language," in *On The Way to Language*, trans. Peter Hertz (New York: Harper & Row, 1982), 57–58. Heidegger's essay makes a useful companion to Emerson's "Experience.".
2. By "Emerson's essays" I mean the essays of the First and Second Series. My references to Emerson's essays (identified in the text, and below, by name) are to the Library of America Edition (New York: Library of America, 1983).
3. Ralph Waldo Emerson, "Experience," 473.
4. The phenomenology I provide here is meant to have diagnostic power, to enable diagnostic responses to the various standard criticisms of Emerson's prose. I do not provide such responses to all the criticisms, but I intend what I do to be suggestive of how such responses go.
5. Gottlob Frege, *Foundations of Arithmetic*, trans. J. L. Austin (London: Blackwell, 1953), 71.
6. Frege, *Foundations*, x.
7. Ludwig Wittgenstein, *Tractatus Logico-Philosophicus*, trans. C. K. Ogden (London: Routledge & Kegan Paul, 1922). See 3.3 and following.
8. Wittgenstein, *Tractatus*, 3.326.
9. Wittgenstein, *Tractatus*, 3.324.
10. *Being and Time*, trans. John Macqaurrie and Edward Robinson (New York: Harper & Row, 1962), 262.
11. I've taken the term, 'field of consciousness' and the phrase 'lights up a field of consciousness' from Stanley Cavell's inestimable essay, "Austin at Criticism," in *Must We Mean What We Say?*

(Cambridge: Cambridge University Press, 1969), 97–114. However, my use of the term and phrase is not entirely Cavell's. In particular, I want 'consciousness' to say 'conscience' *sotto voce*, and not just because of the etymological tie between the words. A field of consciousness is at once a mode of access to what is real and a mode of access to what is valuable. For Emerson, the more consciousness the more conscience, and vice versa. (Despite my departures, I trust that my deep indebtedness to Cavell's writing on Emerson shows itself on each page of this essay.)

12. Emerson, "Intellect," 427.
13. T. S. Eliot, "Lancelot Andrewes," in *Selected Essays: New Edition* (New York: Harcourt, Brace & Company, 1950), 289–300.
14. Eliot, "Lancelot Andrewes," 293.
15. One important discipline of Emersonian quotation is what I call Emersonian *displacement*. To displace is to adjust a formulaic or abstract structure to a roughly credible context. When Emerson quotes, say, Plato or Plotinus or Kant, he takes a formulaic or abstract structure from their thinking on board. He will then, almost without fail, find a place later in the essay in which to displace the structure: he'll find a way to render the structure realistic or plausible. (He also does this to his own original formulaic or abstract structures.)
16. Emerson recontextualizes in other ways, too, of course. But this is his typical way of doing it.
17. One convenience of "Experience" is that in it Emerson collects and lists some of his own essay's elemental terms. He does so both in the preludial poem and in the first sentence of the final section. I take neither list to be exhaustive of the elemental words of the essay, but instead to be exemplary. (Another elemental word of the essay, not listed, is 'middle'.)
18. I take "Experience" to be related to the rest of Emerson's essays as Jesus' Parable of the Sower is related to his other parables. In Mark 4, Jesus tells the Parable, and then complains to his disciples (4:13): "Know ye not this parable? And how then will ye know all parables?" The Sower is the Parable Parable; Emerson's "Experience" is the Essay Essay.
19. See Stanley Cavell, "Aversive Thinking: Emersonian Representations in Heidegger and Nietzsche," in *Emerson's Transcendental Etudes* (Stanford, CA: Stanford University Press, 2003), 141–70.
20. Emerson's "Patience and patience, we shall win at the last," especially in its context, figures Emerson as Job. A fit figuring, it strikes me, for the author of an essay on undergoing, suffering. (Consider: "All I know is reception." Who is speaking? Ralph Waldo or Job? "The Lord giveth, the Lord hath taken away." "The merit itself, so-called, I reckon part of the receiving.") "Experience" has *Job* functioning as both an internal and external scheme. The sections of the essay are rough counterparts to the speeches of the comforters in *Job*; we might call the sections of "Experience" the speeches of the discomforters. The last section, the Coda, is a fairly polished counterpart of the final sections and Coda of *Job*—in which, respectively, God speaks to Job from the Whirlwind, and Job regains his flocks and sons and daughters. "Experience" ends with Emerson speaking from the whirlwind, and promising us that we can self-recover, regain our lost experience. (Does Emerson regain his son? His son's death? Neither?)
21. I'm reading Kant as a two-worlds theorist instead of as a dual-aspect theorist. I judge the former to be the more common reading, although it is not ultimately the reading I favor.
22. Emerson, "Experience," 478.
23. My discussion here is much indebted to discussions of Samuel Todes in *Body and World* (Cambridge, MA: MIT Press, 2001), 38ff.
24. Emerson, "Circles," 406.

The Concept of Writing, with Continual Reference to "Kierkegaard"

~ Mark Cortes Favis ~

Abstract *This essay explores the role that writing plays within the philosophy of Søren Kierkegaard. Given that a majority of his commentators seemingly agree that his philosophy is thoroughly "Socratic," emphasis on what Mallarmé once called the "insane game of writing" perhaps shows that this claim is somewhat inaccurate. For if the Socratic logos is defined according to the proximity of living speech, then the fact that Kierkegaard was, above anything else, a writer would perhaps position him much closer to Plato than to Socrates. This becomes all the more evident when considering what Kierkegaard called the "poet-dialectician," which is indeed a name that is somewhat paradoxical given that it signifies the Socratic philosopher who must engage in those activities which Socrates himself—notably in Plato's Phaedrus—had disparaged as removed from the essence of truth: namely, to write and to poetise. So if Kierkegaard's philosophy is really Socratic in nature, how can he resemble such a "pure thinker" who never wrote a single word?*

Søren Kierkegaard's abounding corpus of writing presumably earns its own unique place within the canon of Western philosophy. His works are formally and thematically varied, ranging from fictional dialogues about aesthetics to solemn treatises concerning religion. Thus, the question arises as to how one characterises Kierkegaard not only with regard to his role as an impassioned philosopher or devout Christian, but also as a poet or writer whose works, he would paradoxically proclaim, proceed *without authority.*[1] The import of the act of writing within Kierkegaard's work cannot be underestimated. As he remarks in an 1848 journal entry: "Assigned from childhood to a life of torment that perhaps few can even conceive of, plunged into the deepest despondency, and from this despondency again into despair, *I came to understand myself by writing.*"[2] This arousal of self-awareness by way of the written word has led many commentators to attribute a presumably *Socratic* meaning—i.e., being of the Socratic ethos or method—to Kierkegaard's distinct mode of

~

philosophical writing. Allegedly analogous to the ways of Socrates, Kierkegaard develops a knack for "indirect communication," a way of writing which feigns ignorance, champions self-knowledge, epitomises the ironical, and betrays a wicked sense of humour. This, the argument goes, allows for the apt characterisation of his authorship as "Socratic" through and through. However, one cannot help but sense a glaring contradiction (perhaps a hint of irony?) in classifying Kierkegaard's authorship as Socratic. In so far as Socrates himself wrote nothing and would also go so far as to denounce writing as removed from the living essence of reason and truth, how could Kierkegaard's writings ever espouse the virtues of a "pure thinker" such as Socrates? When Kierkegaard confesses that "fundamentally, to be an author has been my only possibility," is he not like those poets of Plato's *Republic* who should be forever banned from the philosopher's city?[3]

My essay contends that while it may be partially accurate to portray Kierkegaard as a Socratic thinker, one must also reckon with the notion that his writings are, in a contrasting sense, *Platonic*. In other words: Kierkegaard's *actual, living existence*—i.e., the "Socratic"—as situated within the culture of nineteenth-century Denmark cannot be divorced from (nor purely identified with) his *poetic, authorial existence*—i.e., the "Platonic"—as situated within a world of writing and texts that stretches beyond the spatiotemporal confines of his living existence. Kierkegaard characterises his inward, dialectical existence as it relates to his external, "penned" existence with a term which seemingly holds together these dichotomous Socratic and Platonic points of view: namely, the *poet-dialectician*. The first half of my analysis focuses on the "existence-dialectic" peculiar to Kierkegaard's "Socratic point of view": the element which is recalcitrant towards the written word and prizes, in turn, a true, living subjectivity—what Kierkegaard calls "the single individual." The second half explores his "poetic-existence" specific to his "Platonic point of view": the opposing element that cherishes the creative necessity and stylistic import of the written word, which, as thoroughly poetic, illuminates the authentic *possibilities* inherent to human existence. My essay concludes with how these two modes of existence tarry with each other, at times conflict with one another in an ironical fashion, and, in the end, serve to inform and make up a philosophical activity which not only stays true to the Socratic ideal of an *art of living* but also, and just as importantly, to the corresponding Platonic ideal of a singular and creative *art of writing*. As one of Kierkegaard's literary creations, Johannes Climacus, tells us: "The subjective thinker is not a scientist-scholar, *he is an artist. To exist is an art.*"[4] Prior to unravelling the significance of such an axiom, one must first contend with the notion that this "subjective thinker" Climacus speaks of—as well as how it pertains to Kierkegaard himself as a writer—is somehow "Socratic" in nature.

The argument claiming that Kierkegaard's work as an author is methodically Socratic centres around the notion of "indirect communication": a way of arousing self-awareness—notably that one is ignorant of the truth of one's essential self—not through a direct missive of any kind, but through an ironic deception into the truth. "This in turn is the category," Kierkegaard writes, "of my whole authorship: to *make aware* of the religious, the essentially Christian—but '*without authority*'."[5] Notwithstanding, for now, the precise content of these religious elements, instilling self-awareness without authoritative means requires a peculiar communicative technique, one which skilfully places responsibility for grasping truth, any truth depending on the object, within the interlocutor. Such a technique for Kierkegaard plays an explicit role in his earlier works, the so-called aesthetic writings, which use pseudonymous authors as a way of personifying various categories or "spheres of existence" (mainly the aesthetic, the ethical, and the religious). As incognito and deceptive—what Kierkegaard deems "the deeper significance of the *pseudonymity*"—indirect communication intends to "deceive a person into what is true."[6] The direct method attempts (and mostly fails) to impart a particular truth as if it were a ready-made fact already acceptable as true; the indirect way aims to *remove the delusion* that one already knows the truth, and in turn, aspires to stir a movement towards self-knowledge, to inspire an increasing awareness of the illusions implicit in one's preconceived notions or so-called common sense. This therefore "means that one does not begin *directly* with what one wishes to communicate, but begins by taking the other's delusion at face value."[7] And while the deceiving ways of indirect communication may elicit the thought of swindling the interlocutor into speciousness and falsity, Kierkegaard warns that one should "not be deceived by the word *deception*. One can deceive a person," he continues, "out of what is true, and—*to recall old Socrates*— one can deceive a person into what is true."[8] Indeed, this conjuration of Socrates has led commentators such as Paul Muench to declare that "over the course of [Kierkegaard's] authorship he has employed a Socratic method," one within which "removing illusions, then, facilitates self-knowledge."[9]

The "mask" or "incognito" of Kierkegaard's indirect communication and its underlying mission of removing illusions corresponds to that façade betrayed by Socrates' art of irony—his feigning of ignorance—and its indirect way of leading his interlocutors to the realisation that they, too, are riddled with illusions.[10] Socrates' own indirect communication or "maieutics" nevertheless involves his disguise of ignorance before an interlocutor who, interestingly enough, seeks his knowledge about a particular subject. Whether it concerns piety (e.g., Plato's *Euthyphro*), courage (e.g., *Laches*), virtue (e.g., *Protagoras*), or justice (e.g., *The Republic*), the way in which Socrates ushers the "birth"—by way of an epistemic-existential "midwifery" (e.g., Plato's *Theaetetus*)—to self-awareness and knowledge in his interlocutors involves, in the first instance, his simulation of ignorance, which in turn inspires the interlocutor to proffer unadulterated responses to Socrates' inquiries. However, as the dialectic of questions and answers proceeds, the interlocutor in most cases arrives at the stark realisation that he or she has been deluded all along. Socrates therefore utilises the mask of ignorance to deceive his interlocutors into realising that they are indeed unaware of such and such a matter and should embark, in turn, on the work of self-cultivation that can orient their being towards truth. This communicative method is indeed analogous to Kierkegaard's indirect and deceitful way of arousing awareness in the reader that he or she is not, contrary to initial presumptions, Christian, and must thereby embark on the path of becoming one.

However, the irony of Socratic ignorance highlights a rather significant existential or "inward quality" pertaining to Socrates in his historical actuality. While operating incognito as an ignorant buffoon who was nevertheless sought (and nonetheless executed) for his purported wisdom, his status as a subject, according to the young Kierkegaard, was ironically illuminated. In *The Concept of Irony, with Continual Reference to Socrates*, Kierkegaard contends that Socrates' ironic exterior, his feigning of ignorance, negatively reflects his inward and "unalloyed" subjective existence—his freedom, that is, as a purely "single individual" distinct from the trivialities of the actual and, most of all, the authority of the "crowd."[11] Thoroughly situated within the multicoloured world of Greek culture, Socrates' negative relation to this actuality—his relentless and ironical questioning of the absurdities informing the empirical world—is precisely what grants him freedom as a singular personality par excellence. "In this way," Kierkegaard writes, "he admittedly freed the single individual from every presupposition, freed him as he himself was free; but the freedom he personally enjoyed in ironic satisfaction the other could not enjoy, and thus it developed in them a longing and yearning."[12] Thus, Socrates' ironical stance towards his interlocutors not only serves to arouse the call for self-awareness and self-cultivation; it likewise illumines Socrates' *existential* position as the quintessential singular subject: an ironically created personality freed from—yet negatively remaining a part of—the banality of actual existence. This affirmation of an ironical life thereby underpins Kierkegaard's own "ironical destruction"—by way of indirect communication—of all dominant forms of abstract philosophy (notably Hegelianism) and sham Christianity that were all and all prevalent and "actual" during his own time.[13]

Thus, what the Socratic form of indirect communication necessitates and presupposes is Socratic *inward subjectivity*: what Climacus calls one's living "existence-actuality"—that which is, in its ironic freedom, "infinitely interested" in existing and becomes, in turn, what it is or is supposed to be by way of the Socratic "existence-dialectic."[14] Elsewhere Kierkegaard names this mode of existence "the single individual": one who recognises the undisputed untruth of "the crowd," "society" as such, the anonymously hegemonic "numerical," and maintains oneself, consequently and in truth, in an infinitely inward relationship towards one's self and one's "spirit" or "daimon."[15] The prophecies of the Oracle at Delphi—one of which, as depicted in Plato's *Apology*, tells of Socrates' pre-eminent wisdom—become something resolutely inward for Socrates. "Instead of the Oracle," Kierkegaard writes, "Socrates now has his daimon. The daimonian in this case now lies in the transition from the Oracle's external relation to the individual to *the complete inwardness of freedom*."[16] This relationship-in-freedom compares analogously to Kierkegaard's own "God-relationship": an inwardly religious association that not only justifies his own singular individuality, but is precisely that "happy love of [his] unhappy and troubled life" which helped "to defend [himself] against the abundance of thoughts."[17] In the end, it is this exaltation of one's infinite inward subjectivity that Kierkegaard finds most noteworthy of a philosopher such as Socrates.

Despite these apparent similarities between the indirect methods of Socrates and Kierkegaard, it is perhaps this very notion of one's inward, subjective existence that anchors an irrevocable separation and distinction between the Socratic and Kierkegaardian modes of philosophical communication. While someone like Benjamin Daise purports that Kierkegaard's form of indirect communication is a mere modification of its Socratic form (and is therefore a "Socratic art"),[18] the category of the inwardly-subsisting single individual corresponds primarily, for Socrates, to the communicative form or *logos* of *living speech*: intimate dialogue or dialectics.[19] This, in my view, presents a remarkable difference that is often overlooked by Kierkegaard's commentators. Socrates' argument, for instance, in Plato's *Phaedrus*—a dialogue about the merits of rhetoric and speechwriting—appears to strike wholeheartedly against Kierkegaard's entire endeavour regardless if his authorship is characterised as "aesthetic," "religious," or otherwise.

Thus, if one is to believe Kierkegaard's claim that "fundamentally, to be an author has been [his] only possibility,"[20] then the Socratic "point of view" remains arguably and intrinsically antithetical to such an authorship and to such a possibility.

> Therefore, he [the writer] won't be serious about writing them [e.g., his subject-matter] in ink, sowing them, through pen, with *words that are incapable of speaking in their own defence as they are of teaching the truth adequately.*[21]

The concluding passages to Plato's *Phaedrus* provide the quintessential example of how Socrates' indiscriminate admonition of writing creates an immeasurable gulf between him and Kierkegaard.[22] Writing, according to Socrates, is an art form of mere "imagery" that is far removed from the living essence of the philosophical art of dialectics; the latter is, according to Socrates' interlocutor—Phaedrus—the "living, breathing discourse of the man who knows":[23] a form of communication that is radically opposed to the purported *exteriority* of the written word. At one point in the dialogue, Socrates recalls an Egyptian fable illustrating the discovery of writing: Thamus, king of Egypt, purportedly tells Thoth, the god of wisdom, science, and writing that the written word "will introduce forgetfulness in the soul" in so far as it is "external and depends on signs that belong to others."[24] Such exteriority prevents the writer from remembering "from the inside"—that is, from being present and in touch with the inwardness of one's soul. The "existence actuality" or "inward subjectivity" that is indicative of the figure of Socrates is therefore fundamentally belied, confuted, and offended by the communicative form of writing. And while the Socrates of Plato's *The Republic* deprecates the fine artist of any genre as a mere "imitator" or "image-maker" who not only "stands far removed from the truth,"[25] but who also represents some kind of aesthetic terrorist to be banished from the philosopher's city, Socrates in Plato's *Phaedrus* makes a similar indictment against writing:

> You know, Phaedrus, writing shares a strange feature with painting. The offspring of painting stand there as if they are alive, but if anyone asks them anything, they remain solemnly silent. The same is true of written words.... When it has once been written down, every discourse roams everywhere, reaching indiscriminately those with understanding no less than those with no business with it, and it doesn't know to whom it should speak and to whom it should not. And when it is faulted and attacked unfairly, it always needs its father's support; alone, it can neither defend itself nor come to its own support.[26]

What, then, are we to say about Kierkegaard's "point of view of his work as an author?" Is it possible that Kierkegaard's form of "indirect *writing*" is diametrically opposed to Socrates' "indirect *speech*" in so far as the true dialectician, the one who lives and breathes his or her *logos*, "chooses a proper soul and plants and sows within it a [spoken] discourse accompanied by knowledge?"[27] How does one's inward, subjective existence relate—if possible—to that form of art which produces a discourse that is merely external, solely a dead image or sign, and is perhaps a menacing "phantom?"[28] The following epigraph appears to betray Kierkegaard's allegiance with Socrates' denunciation of the written word:

> If in nothing else, on this point I truly believe that I have something in common with Socrates. Just as the daimon of Socrates, when Socrates was accused and about to be

sentenced by "the crowd," he who felt himself to be a divine gift, forbade himself to *defend* himself—indeed, what an impropriety and self-contradiction it would have been!—so also there is in me and in the dialectical nature of my relationship something that makes it impossible for me and impossible in itself to conduct a 'defence' of my authorship.[29]

That which lies within Kierkegaard himself and within his dialectical relationship with his "daimon" (or God) is precisely that which precludes any chance of "defending" his authorship as such. The Socrates of Plato's *Phaedrus* indeed provides part of the reason for why the writer can never be present to a discourse that indiscriminately "roams everywhere" and is without its "father's support"—the writer is, as Hélène Cixous once remarked, a "homeless virgin." However, given that Socrates would reduce writing to the allegedly shameful and characteristic mimicry of the fine arts in general, Kierkegaard's confessed inability to defend his authorship does not at all result in a Socratic disparagement of writing. His claim that the "difficulty in publishing anything about the authorship" derives from the fact that he, as an inwardly existing individual, "cannot, after all, say: *I.*"[30] This assertion in fact leads, contra Socrates, to a particular *reverence* for writing as a necessary "mode of existence" containing its own peculiar truth. This truth persists regardless of the author's sheepish failure to provide any testimony or defence for his or her own discourse. Given that Kierkegaard's doctoral dissertation follows the "concept of irony with continual reference to Socrates," there is also a recurrent allusion to the *writer's* responsibility towards the possible inheritance of a Socratic way of philosophising. Not only does Kierkegaard prize Plato's "free poetising" of Socrates as well as Aristophanes' rendering of the philosopher into comic relief, but his treatise also concludes with ruminations over the function of irony (as a "controlled element") within literary writing.[31] In the end, Kierkegaard's characterisation of irony is equally pertinent to the poetic mode of writing itself.

Kierkegaard's preference for the *literary* interpretations of Socrates as opposed to those dry and "objective" renditions belonging to Xenophon harbours its own peculiar irony, one which also illuminates Kierkegaard's early appraisal of poetic inscription. Throughout the first part of *The Concept of Irony* ("The Position of Socrates Viewed as Irony"), Kierkegaard announces his desire to find "a reliable and authentic view of Socrates' historical–actual, phenomenological existence."[32] "This becomes inescapably necessary," according to Kierkegaard, "because the concept of irony makes its entry into the world through Socrates" (9). Of the three surviving accounts of Socrates, Kierkegaard chastises the author who perhaps provides a more objective account of Socrates in so far as he refrains from any use of literary device or stylistic overture. In Xenophon "we found Socrates busily functioning as an apostle of finitude, as an officious bagman for mediocrity [who valued] the useful rather than the good, the useful rather than the beautiful, the established rather than the true" (127). And the reason why this Socrates of "Xenophon's puppet box" belies any historical truth and validity is due primarily to the author's vacuous style of writing, its painstaking ennui, one which espouses a "total lack of situation"—a decolouring of Ancient Greek culture—and presents, furthermore, the Socratic dialectic as a movement "just as invisible and shallow a straight line, just as monotonous as the single-colour background that children and Nurnberg painters customarily use in their pictures" (16). This undeniably reflects the problem of form and style—a disheartening ignorance of the import of writing; and it is also an issue which Plato's poetic productions and Aristophanes' comic plays appear to rectify. The irony therefore lies in the fact that a literary and seemingly "fictional" way of writing can most plausibly grant access to the historical and "unalloyed Socrates" (40).

Part of the reason why Plato, more so than Xenophon, provides a more accurate portrayal of Socrates is due to his poetic rendering of his mentor. Kierkegaard reminds us "that it was from a productive life as a poet that Socrates called the twenty-year-old Plato back to abstract knowledge" (105). Plato can indeed be credited for poetically interpreting Socrates as he was in his *situated* existence (i.e., as part of the hustle and bustle of Greek life); he can also be lauded for illustrating an ironical personality whose feigned ignorance and engaged "midwifery" served to further the project and purpose of philosophy and the overall pursuit of knowledge. However, he had also introduced a *mythical* element into his Socratic dialogues (notably in the earlier works, such as *The Symposium*) as a way of illustrating what was mysterious, paradoxical, and ironic about Socrates' teachings. "In the mythical part of the *Symposium*," for example, "Plato the *poet* daydreams and visualises everything the *dialectician* Socrates was seeking; in the world of dreams, irony's unhappy love finds its object" (108). In so far as "the mythical is the enthusiasm of the imagination in service of speculation," its strictly poetic features lie in the skilled use of metaphor (101). Socrates' ironical existence therefore necessitated the poet's use of metaphor, mythical storytelling, and other such devices since no *direct* communication or "objective" interpretation—such as that of Xenophon's "puppet box"—would suffice to accurately portray such a figure.

Additionally, Aristophanes' comedies succeed in this regard given that they make Socrates into a "comic character" whose personality and ironic subjectivity are negatively displayed (128); for to simply "apprehend the empirical actuality of Socrates, to bring him on stage as he walked and stood in life, would have been beneath the dignity of Aristophanes" (129). Instead, and contrary to what Socrates says about that "necessary evil" known as writing, a literary form of communication would indeed be necessary vis-à-vis any attempt to portray the actual, inward existence of an ironical subject such as Socrates. Such a relation, then, between the *personal* and the *poetical* is encapsulated in what Kierkegaard calls the "poet-dialectician":

> [T]he poet or, more accurately, *the poet-dialectician*, does not make himself out to be the ideal and even less does he judge any single human being. But he holds up the ideal so that everyone, if he has a mind to, in quiet solitariness can compare his own life with the ideal.[33]

This title of the "poet-dialectician" aptly represents the opposing characteristics of the philosopher-as-writer: the one who exists inwardly as a living subject and the one who exists externally as a writing/written subject. The *dialectical* element of one's inward existence refers to the human ideal of Socrates (i.e., of the ironical positing of the free individual) or the "supreme" ideal of Jesus Christ (i.e., of becoming a Christian).[34] The *poetical* feature, on the other hand, of one's external, "writerly" existence aims for the free and authentic creation, presentation, and communication (*logos*) of this ideal to oneself and to others. The style of the poet-dialectician—as the holding-together of the Socratic and Platonic modes—thoroughly characterises Kierkegaard's work as both a philosopher and writer who, through painstaking effort, studied the lived joys and tried tribulations of human existence. Above all, as the pseudonym Johannes Climacus writes, "the subjective thinker's task is to *understand himself in existence*."[35] Such an understanding, for Kierkegaard as an author, happens inwardly (i.e., religiously or Socratically) inasmuch as it is created and exhibited outwardly by way of the written word.

This title of "subjective thinker" used by Climacus is arguably synonymous with that of the "poet-dialectician." For Climacus, the subjective thinker is ultimately a "dialectician oriented to the existential; he has the intellectual passion to hold firm the qualitative disjunction" which persists among the spheres of existence. This "absolute disjunction" is nothing less than those extreme opposites of the poetical and personal, those which equally require—in addition to intellectual zeal—an "aesthetic passion and ethical [or religious] passion, whereby concretion [in existence] is gained." Hence why characteristics indicative of the poetical—"imagination" and "feeling"—are just as necessary for the subjective thinker as "dialectics in impassioned existence-inwardness"— that which receives its justification, as noted above, through one's inward confessions to God (350).[36] Hence also why Kierkegaard via Climacus would go to great lengths to distinguish this bifurcated identity of the poet-dialectician from the artist, ethicist, or priest; the subjective thinker, in other words, is never purely identified with one or the other alone. The poet-dialectician, writes Climacus, "is not a poet even if he is also a poet, not an ethicist if he is also an ethicist, but is also a dialectician and is himself essentially existing" (351). In the end, the subjective thinker's poetical form must at all times be related to one's personal existence; it must therefore be "as manifold as are the opposites he holds together" (357). Although one's personal and poetical existence must be held together in some such way within the poet-dialectician, the personal can never in its concrete actuality be imparted as such. One's inward "existence-actuality cannot be communicated," Climacus writes, in so far as actuality must always "be understood as *possibility*, and a communicator who is conscious of this will therefore see to it, precisely in order to be oriented to existence, *that his existence-communication is in the form of possibility*" (358, emphasis added). In so far, then, as one's "existence-actuality" may perhaps find inward expression through one's confessions to God, the articulation of existence or *possibility* as such is best communicated by way of the poetic word. "Poetry," for Climacus—and, for that matter, for Kierkegaard himself—"has possibility at its disposal" (318). As Aristotle once put it:

> [T]he function of the poet is not to say what *has* happened, but to say the kind of thing that *would* happen, i.e., what is possible in accordance with probability or necessity. . . . For this reason poetry is more philosophical and more serious than history. Poetry tends to express universals, and history particulars. The *universal* is the kind of speech or action which is consonant with a person of a given kind in accordance with probability or necessity; this is what poetry aims at.[37]

Thus, while commentators such as Muench argue that Climacus is a "thoroughly Socratic figure" in so far as, "like Socrates, his principal target is a certain kind of blameworthy *ignorance* . . . of which he seeks to make his interlocutors aware" by way of "maieutic techniques," such a claim must necessarily be supplemented by the *Platonic* or *poetic* elements that are thoroughly antithetical to the Socratic *logos*.[38] The latter pertains to the living situation of actual existence—what Kierkegaard considers as "inward"— where the dialectics of the spoken word are purportedly valued in their proximity to the essence of truth. The former, on the other hand, relates to a poetical or pseudonymous existence which perhaps harbours a "maieutics" peculiar to the written or graphic *logos*. While it is relatively indisputable that Kierkegaard's indirect communication—or, as Paul Muench and James Conant prefer, his "art of 'taking away'"—is designed, like Socratic discourse, to remove the reader's delusions and to make one aware of one's own ignorance, its written and poetic dimension—i.e., the subjective thinker's *style*—perhaps carries a function peculiar to itself.

Judging by the way several commentators react to Kierkegaard's writing hints at the creative import indicative of the poet–dialectician's style. Clare Carlisle, for instance, asks if "to study for or to teach a university course, to produce a PhD thesis, [or] to write about Kierkegaard" is perhaps antithetical as a reader's response to what is demanded by Kierkegaard's writings: "Do these approaches conflict with the movement of inward reflection that all Kierkegaard's texts, pseudonymous and overtly religious, prompt us to make?"[39] In addition to his works' purported Socratic function, perhaps there is equally a Platonic function that arouses "imagination," "feeling," and passion within one's own writing—those which are all too often lost within the demands of academic scripture? As Conant wittily remarks in his essay on Kierkegaard and Wittgenstein: "An academic author writing something which has the form of a conventional scholarly essay ... is apt to be struck by some of the ways in which the literary structure of his own performance is at odds with what these authors themselves have to say." And hence the obvious truism that "no sooner does one begin than one has already failed them."[40] What such comments merely allude to is the seemingly Platonic or poetic demand that, vis-à-vis one's inward existence, one's presentation or production assumes "the form of possibility."[41] The reader may not only be called upon, in the Socratic sense, to question the delusions present within one's personal existence; one may also, Platonically speaking, be induced to address one's own creative impulses in so far as they correspond to the movement of *possibility*, of "becoming," which in itself characterises the very mode of human existence. Thus, concludes Climacus:

> In the form of possibility, the presentation becomes a requirement. Instead of presenting the good in the form of actuality, *as is ordinarily done, that this person and that person have actually lived and have actually done this*, and thus transforming the reader into an observer, an admirer, an appraiser [and even a commentator!], it should be presented in the form of possibility. Then whether or not the reader wants to exist in it is placed as possible to him.[42]

While one may be ultimately tempted to follow Kierkegaard's unremitting claims of analogy and resemblance between himself and Socrates as a sign that his existence qua *writer* is intrinsically Socratic, it is glaringly evident that the *art of writing* itself—the Platonic element—precludes any strict identity between the two. Kierkegaard's status as a philosophical writer—as the *poet-dialectician* par excellence—must account for the Platonic appraisal of writing that accompanies and necessarily communicates any semblance of a Socratic or Christian art of inward existence. As noted earlier, the Socratic mode of "indirect communication" is contingent upon an interpretation of the philosophical *logos*—that bounded sphere of expressivity: a "discourse"—which is, for Socrates, unavoidably live, proximal, and present to itself as such. This "existence-dialectic" for Kierkegaard is grounded in his religious practice, his personal existence, where this inwardly "present" discourse between him and God (his "God-relationship") justifies his authentic individuality. The latter signifies his status as a "single individual" which in turn and in principle remains inaccessible to the reader due to its silent and irrevocable secrecy. This inaccessibility to Kierkegaard's inward, dialectical existence is complemented by the "Platonic *logos*," which, as characteristically poetic, is seemingly recalcitrant to the primacy of living speech. Contra Socrates, Kierkegaard's authorship prizes the necessity for poetic expression, for a free stylisation of one's existence-as-possibility by way of the written word. Thus, while the Socratic element calls for self-awareness of one's own inward becoming within the stream of living existence, the Platonic element arouses the self-awareness of one's stylistic capacities, of one's need to communicate one's self—as *possibility*—playfully if not ironically by way of poetics and an inventive "self-writing."[43]

It could also be argued that Kierkegaard seemingly predates the postmodern (or "post-mortem") notion of the "Death of the Author."[44] For him, one's inward existence cannot attend to or be captured by written discourse—a truth which should not, following Socrates, be received with lament and renunciation. Instead, the poetic *logos* should be embraced as a way of experimenting with the self as well as a way of communicating—as undoubtedly "indirect"—the aesthetic and spiritual import of this kind of play. Given this essay's introductory epigraph featured Hélène Cixous's picturesque line expressing the resultant homelessness of the one who writes, concluding with a Kierkegaardian "axiom" appears fitting:

> But this is my limitation—I am a pseudonym. Fervently, incitingly, I present the ideal, and when the listener or reader is moved to tears, then I still have one job left: to say, "I am not that, my life is not like that."[45]

Notes

I am deeply grateful to Lisa Damon, Michelle Favis, Daniel Watts, and Béatrice Han–Pile for their thoughts and comments on this essay.

1. Søren Kierkegaard, "On My Work as an Author," in *The Point of View*, trans. H. V. and E. H. Hong (Princeton, NJ: Princeton University Press, 1998), 6.
2. Kierkegaard, "Supplement: Selected Entries from Kierkegaard's Journals and Papers Pertaining to *On My Work as an Author* and *The Point of View for My Work as an Author*," in *The Point of View*, 162, emphasis added.
3. *Ibid.*, 212.
4. Søren Kierkegaard, *Concluding Unscientific Postscript to Philosophical Fragments*, trans. H. V. Hong and E. H. Hong (Princeton, NJ: Princeton University Press, 1992), 351, emphasis added.
5. Kierkegaard, "On My Work as an Author," 6.
6. Kierkegaard, "The Point of View for My Work as an Author," 24 and 53, respectively.
7. *Ibid.*, 54.
8. *Ibid.*, 53, emphasis added.
9. Paul Muench, "Kierkegaard's Socratic Task" (PhD diss., University of Pittsburgh, 2006), 22 and 40, respectively.
10. Regarding Socratic irony, see Alexander Nehamas's second chapter in *The Art of Living: Socratic Reflections from Plato to Foucault* (Berkeley, CA: University of California Press, 2000).

Regarding the Socratic method, see Pierre Hadot, "The Figure of Socrates," in *Philosophy as a Way of Life*, trans. A. I. Davidson (Oxford: Blackwell, 1995).

11. Søren Kierkegaard, *The Concept of Irony with Continual Reference to Socrates*, trans. H. V. and E. H. Hong (Princeton, NJ: Princeton University Press, 1989), Part 1.

12. *Ibid.*, 176.

13. This view is indeed epitomised by the pseudonym Johannes Climacus in *Concluding Unscientific Postscript*.

14. See Chapter 3, "Actual Subjectivity, Ethical Subjectivity; the Subjective Thinker," of Kierkegaard's pseudonymous work *Concluding Unscientific Postscript*.

15. Kierkegaard, "'The Single Individual' – Two 'Notes' Concerning My Work as an Author," in *The Point of View*, 105–12.

16. Kierkegaard, *The Concept of Irony*, 163–64.

17. Kierkegaard, "Governance's Part in My Authorship," in *The Point of View*, 71 and 74, respectively.

18. See Benjamin Daise, *Kierkegaard's Socratic Art* (Macon, GA: Mercer University Press, 1999). Also consider Mark C. Taylor's second chapter to his *Kierkegaard's Pseudonymous Authorship: A Study of Time and the Self* (Princeton, NJ: Princeton University Press, 1975).

19. Regarding the interpretation of the *logos* as "live speech," see Adriana Cavarero, *For More Than One Voice: Toward a Philosophy of Vocal Expression*, trans. P. A. Kottman (Stanford, CA: Stanford University Press, 2005).

20. Kierkegaard, "Supplement: Selected Entries," 212.

21. Plato, "Phaedrus," *Plato: Complete Works*, trans. A. Nehamas and P. Woodruff, ed. J. M. Cooper (Indianapolis, IN: Hackett Publishing, 1997), l. 276c, emphasis added.

22. Jacques Derrida excavates the fullest implications of the denunciation of writing that pervades the entire philosophical tradition since Socrates. See his reading of Plato's *Phaedrus* in *Dissemination*, trans. B. Johnson (London: Continuum, 2004). For an interesting comparative reading—which, in my view, could be supplemented with an emphasis on the art of writing—between Derrida and Kierkegaard concerning the problem of "origins" in metaphysics, see Michael Weston's *Kierkegaard and Modern Continental Philosophy: An Introduction* (London: Routledge, 1994).

23. Plato, "Phaedrus," l. 276a.

24. *Ibid.*, l. 275a.

25. Plato, *The Republic*, trans. T. Griffith (Cambridge: Cambridge University Press, 2000), ll. 605b–c.

26. Plato, "Phaedrus," ll. 275d–e.

27. *Ibid.*, l. 276e.

28. Another translation of Plato's *Phaedrus* interprets "image" as a kind of "ghost" or "spectre": i.e., "written speech would rightly be called a kind of phantom." See Plato, *Phaedrus*, trans. C. Rowe (London: Penguin Classics, 2005), l. 276a.

29. Kierkegaard, "The Point of View of My Work as an Author," 24.

30. Kierkegaard, "Supplement: About the Completed Unpublished Writings and Myself," in *The Point of View*, 209.

31. Kierkegaard, *The Concept of Irony*, 31.

32. Kierkegaard, *The Concept of Irony*, 9; subsequent page references are cited in the text.

33. Kierkegaard, "Armed Neutrality," in *The Point of View*, 133, emphasis added.

34. In a postscript to his essays on the model of the single individual, Kierkegaard writes that "Jesus Christ, to name the *supreme* example, truth itself, certainly had followers; and, to name a *human* example, Socrates had followers." See his "Postscript to 'Two Notes',," in *Point of View*, 125, emphasis added.

35. Kierkegaard, *Concluding Unscientific Postscript*, 351; subsequent page references are cited in the text.

36. Regarding the role of the imagination in Kierkegaard's work, see Sylvia Walsh, "Kierkegaard: Poet of the Religious," in *Kierkegaard on Art and Communication*, ed. G. Pattison (New York: St. Martin's Press, 1992), 1–22.

37. Aristotle, *Poetics*, trans. M. Heath (London: Penguin, 1996), l. 9; 51a–b.
38. Paul Muench, "The Socratic Method of Kierkegaard's Pseudonym Johannes Climacus: Indirect Communication as the Art of 'Taking Away'," in *Søren Kierkegaard and the Word(s): Essays on Hermeneutics and Communication*, ed. P. Houe and G. D. Marino (Copenhagen: C. A. Reitzel, 2003), 139.
39. Clare Carlisle, *Kierkegaard: A Guide for the Perplexed* (London: Continuum, 2006), 43.
40. James Conant, "Putting Two and Two Together: Kierkegaard, Wittgenstein, and the Point of View of Their Work as Authors," in *The Grammar of Religious Belief*, ed. D. Z. Phillips (New York: St. Martin's Press, 1996), 248.
41. Kierkegaard, *Concluding Unscientific Postscript*, 358.
42. *Ibid.*, 358–59, emphasis added.
43. Michel Foucault, for instance, traces the genealogy of this phenomenon of 'self-writing'—one which has been lost in contemporary philosophy—within the philosophical canon. See Michel Foucault, "Self Writing," in *Ethics: Subjectivity and Truth*, trans. R. Hurley *et al.*, ed. P. Rabinow (London: Penguin, 2000).
44. See Roland Barthes, "Death of the Author," in *Image–Music–Text*, trans. S. Heath (New York: Hill, 1977).
45. Kierkegaard, "Supplement: About the Completed Unpublished Writings and Myself," 210.

An Inhumanly Wise Shame

~ Brendan Moran ~

ABSTRACT   *In Kafka's work, Benjamin detects a gesture of shame, which he characterizes as historico-philosophic (geschichtsphilosophisch). He considers Kafka's gesture of shame to be philosophic in its opposition to myth, which is closure concerning history. In its elaboration of Kafka's gesture, moreover, Benjamin's analysis itself becomes a gesture of shame and thus somehow "literary." This does not detract from the notion that the gesture—in Kafka's work and in Benjamin's criticism—remains philosophic. Kafka's literary work is philosophic in shaming mythic interpretations of it; Benjamin's philosophic criticism continues this gesture by advancing shame about mythic tendencies either in the work or in its reception. Without pathos, Kafka presents astonished shame at mythic human order and is attentive to exceptions to, deviations from, such order. Benjamin's criticism continues the latter attentiveness, but the attentiveness, the philosophic element in Kafka's literature, is also betrayed by Benjamin in some respects.*

Warum wolle er sich denn nicht fügen?
  —Franz Kafka, *Der Proceß*

In his analyses of Kafka's work, Walter Benjamin rarely uses the term "philosophic" and never uses the noun "philosophy." Yet he characterizes a gesture of shame, which he contends is fundamental in Kafka's work, as historico-philosophic (*geschichtsphilosophisch*). The latter term could be rendered as "philosophical concerning history," and indicates that Benjamin detects in Kafka's works something pertinent to the love of wisdom, to philosophy. The gesture of shame is philosophic in opposing myth, which is closure concerning history. In its elaboration of Kafka's gesture, moreover, Benjamin's analysis itself openly becomes a gesture of shame.

This relationship of philosophy and literature is conceived by Benjamin as a convergence in which Kafka's historico-philosophic shame anticipates its continuance in criticism. The literary work is philosophic in shaming mythic interpretations of it; philosophic criticism continues this gesture by advancing the shame as independent of mythic tendencies either in the work or in its reception. The gesture of shame is not,

~

moreover, the pathos of wonder that is often considered characteristic of the phil⌐
the inextinguishable and inhuman force impelling shame about humans' attachme⌐
to myth indulges no pathos, no anthropomorphic characterization. Only without pathos
can there be Kafka's astonished shame at the mythic character of human order. Only in
this way can Kafka's writings be attentive to the exceptions to, the deviations from, myth.
This philosophic gesture of attentiveness is continued in Benjamin's criticism, although—
as will be elaborated at the close of this study—this attentiveness, this wisdom of Kafka's
literature, is occasionally betrayed by Benjamin.

GESTURE OF PHILOSOPHY

It is uncontroversial to say that "Benjamin's method" is "in no way philosophic in the
conventional sense," but this remark (made in the 1970s) was accompanied by the
contention that Benjamin's "historico-philosophic critique [geschichtsphilosophischen
Kritik]" rejects "interpretative analysis" in favour of an "esoteric," in many respects
"authoritarian," "linguistic gesture [Sprachgestus]."[1] Although Adorno dismisses the view
that Benjamin is a poet and not a philosopher,[2] even he argues that Benjamin has
a tendency (reminiscent of the George-school) towards spell-binding, immobilizing
"philosophical gesturing [Gestik],"[3] a tendency that can become "authoritarian" and is in
need of a more Hegelian deployment of concept.[4] Adorno says that his and Benjamin's
"agreement" in the "philosophical" was clear to him upon reading Benjamin's Kafka-
essay of 1934.[5] Yet Benjamin's Kafka-reading gestures to elements of a preponderant
cloudiness, which Adorno would prefer Benjamin "durchzudialektisieren."[6]

The above objections, along with Adorno's expressly Hegelian criticisms of
the Unfertigkeit (unclosedness) in Benjamin's Kafka-interpretations, may be of limited
relevance to the gesture discerned by Benjamin in Kafka and to the gesture of Benjamin's
reading.[7] If Benjamin's gesture is esoteric, it is so not in the sense of binding itself with
any secret that only adepts can access; neither authoritarian nor immobilizing, it offers
nothing as authority and thereby maintains secret as the interpretative horizon for all.
Benjamin's criticism on Kafka's writings does not abandon the view, expressed in the
Trauerspielbuch, that among the "postulates" of "philosophical style" is the "perseverance
of discourse [Ausdauer der Abhandlung]" in contrast with "the gesture [Geste] of the
fragment" (O, 32/I:1, 212). As distinctly perseverant discourse, philosophy is no fragment
that is to be treated as inviolably apart. Nor can it treat anything else—including the art
work—as inviolably apart. There is no final gesture. Benjamin's characterization of
philosophy as persistently discursive is not incompatible, however, with his attendant
notion of philosophy as Darstellung (performance or presentation), for this concerns
philosophy as a discursive style that openly performs beyond the discursive—beyond
the denotative (and any connoted denotations) (O, 27–28, 32/I:1, 207–8, 212 and
I:3, 925–26).[8] The style could be considered one of philosophy as gesture, for without something like gesture that opens to the non-denotative, "philosophy" would be
something other than love of wisdom.

Agamben accordingly refers to "the silence of philosophy . . . pure gesturality."[9]
Such silence is also evoked in Benjamin's reference to "sound film" as a "limit for the
world of Kafka and Chaplin" (II:3, 1256).[10] In consideration of these statements by

Benjamin and Agamben, it could be proposed that philosophy and art meet in the gesture of silence. Such gesture opens to a "mimetic" medium that is not subordinate to sense (*W* 2, 722/II:1, 213). This opening is "a critical moment" (697–98/209–10), for no meaning can credibly be ascribed to the mimetic gesture. Benjamin associates the "primacy of the gesture" with "its incomprehensibility [*Unverständlichkeit*]" (II:3, 1206).[11] In his short excursus "Kafka Defended Against His Interpreters," Agamben too stresses a priority of the inexplicable.[12] After remarks elsewhere on Benjamin's reading of the gestural in Kafka, moreover, Agamben articulates what could be considered a Benjaminian notion of criticism as philosophy: "Criticism is the reduction of works to the sphere of pure gesture. This sphere lies…, in a certain sense, beyond all interpretation."[13] Criticism must be philosophy as pure gesturality, for such gesture is gesture of the inextinguishable mystery to which any art work opens. Criticism is a continuance of the latter opening. Criticism responds to, and continues, a gesture of speechlessness in response to an emptiness that cannot be filled.[14]

Endeavouring to fill the emptiness would be shameless. Kafka liberates shame about such endeavours.[15] Benjamin's Kafka-readings renew and regenerate this liberated shame. Perhaps Benjamin had this in mind when he referred to his work on Kafka as dealing with "two ends simultaneously": "the political" and "the mystical" (*C*, 458/*GB* IV, 513–14). If the mystical is refusal to fill the emptiness, Benjamin's correlative criticism is an ever-renewable continuance of the art work's shame about endeavours to fill the emptiness. Such critical gesture becomes what Agamben refers to as a "politics" that has also been called "philosophy."[16]

WISE SHAME

Benjamin's critical-philosophical exercise is expressly an attempt to respond to Kafka's gesture, which Benjamin considers to be ultimately removed from any affect and indeed from any interpretative sense (II:3, 1201, 1229).[17] Benjamin's criticism is conceived as a response to the way in which Kafka's works often sap the portrayed occurrences of their sense and thereby let "gestural content" emerge "more sharply" (II:3, 1229). By divesting "human gesture of its traditional supports," Kafka opens gesture to potentially interminable interpretation or consideration (*W* 2, 802/II:2, 420; II:3, 1229). By so opening itself to study, gesture defies myth, which is closure of interpretation. To illustrate a "Chinese wisdom" in Kafka's writings, Benjamin notes the studying by the horse Bucephalus, by Sancho Panza, and by Karl (whose boyhood studying is recalled in *Der Verschollene* [Amerika]); this studying is (to borrow Rosenzweig's terms) very close to the nothing that alone makes it possible for a something to be useful—that is, the studying is close to the Tao (II:3, 1243 and *W* 2, 813/II:434–35). The Taoist gesture, the "Chinese" wisdom, in Kafka becomes Benjamin's own to the extent that Benjamin's reading respects this nothing by never closing off consideration of it (813/435).[18]

A complication seems, however, to arise. The gesture of nothing is supposedly devoid of affect and yet is also "shame," which is conventionally regarded as an emotion, a psychological feeling, an affect.[19] Even some very careful studies of the gestural in Benjamin's Kafka-writings do not address this seemingly awkward development that the gesture is identified with shame.[20] With regard to mourning, Benjamin's *Trauerspielbuch* had nonetheless already addressed "a feeling [*Fühlen*] removed from the empirical subject" (*O*, 139/I:1, 318). Somewhat in this vein, Deleuze and Guattari contend that a powerful impetus for philosophy is a deterritorializing feeling, which they characterize as shame of being human.[21]

Not dissimilarly, Benjamin registers the shame in Kafka's writings as irreducible to conceivable meanings. The shame corresponds with Kafka's "'elemental purity of feeling.'" This expression is openly an adaptation of Rosenzweig's portrayal of a "Chinese" propensity for a feeling devoid of individual character. Rosenzweig considers the "Chinese" inwardness so tenuously connected to the outward that it results in people seeming simply "the average person" (*Durchschnittsmensch*). More favourably, Benjamin wonders if this turning away from outwardly communicating properties is the gesture in Kafka's works, as evidenced in the way Kafka's Theatre of Oklahoma dissolves "events into the gestural" (*W* 2, 801/II:2, 418).[22] Kafka's "strongest gesture" is the shame that is a thoroughly impersonal inability to rest with meanings (*W* 2, 808/II:2, 428). The strength of the gesture may seem a weak strength or a strong weakness, not unlike Hölderlin's "Timidness" (*Blödigkeit*) that is inexhaustible in having no realization (*W* 1, 18–36/II:1, 105–26). In presenting Kafka's gesture of shame as without affect, Benjamin conceives of the "Vorwelt"—the world withstanding myth, "Kafka's secret present [*geheime Gegenwart*]"—as the "historico-philosophical index [*der geschichtsphiloso-phische Index*]" that takes the "reaction" of shame out of the "realm of the private constitution." Not strictly shame that one might feel as personal shame (as shame about oneself in relation to other human beings), the gesture emerges as philosophic shame about human history—about laws or any other measures that indicate a presumption to deal with, somehow overcome, the "Vorwelt" (*C*, 453/*GB* IV, 478/II:3, 1165). This "Vorwelt" is secret; it manifests itself only as what cannot be made manifest. The only common dimension—that is, the only epic dimension—is this *Vorwelt* that remains secret (*W* 2, 797, 807, 809/II:2, 412, 426–27, 429).[23] Indeed, Kafka's gesture would be entirely secret if not for its shame about all that is oblivious to secret. The shame impels the performance of secret as secret. This gesture of shame is advanced by Benjamin as wise—philosophic, in a quasi-Taoist way (*W* 2, 799, 815/II:2, 415, 437).[24]

In accordance with the gesture of shame, Kafka's poetic prohibition on graven images (*W* 2, 808/II:2 428) also prohibits any claim to succeed in interpreting Kafka. In this sense at least, there is no key that can be provided for what Kafka writes (II:3, 1218). "Kafka's entire work" presents "a codex of gestures that in no way have an inherently definite symbolic meaning" (*W* 2, 801/II:2, 418).[25] The "symbolic content" (symbolisher Gehalt) or "symbol" prevails instead as "gesture" (Gestus) over any "teaching content" (Lehrgehalt), any parable (Gleichnis) (II:3, 1255). In Kafka's gesture, any quest for teaching finds its failure to be necessary (II:3, 1250, II:3, 1253–54).[26] The poetic gesture is this failure: Kafka "regarded his efforts as unsuccessful; ... he counted himself among those who had to fail. Failed is his magnificent attempt to lead poetry [*Dichtung*] into teaching [*Lehre*] and to give back to it—as parable—the long-lastingness and unpretentiousness [*Unscheinbarkeit*] which, in the face of reason, appeared to him as the only appropriate approach" (*W* 2, 807–8/II:2, 427–28). The quest for doctrine or teaching (*Lehre*) wants something durable, something so right that there will be no chance of it seeming pretentious or conspicuous. This quest is so powerful in Kafka that it passes beyond its content and into a void. "[C]ontemplation" (*Betrachtung*) enters "heights" that require "parable [*Parabel*]" to cast aside its "material [*Stoff*]" (II:3, 1256). The void opened by the mystic, the gesture, the visionary, cannot be closed or filled by parable, instruction, sage (II:3, 1260). Kafka's shame prohibits fulfilment of expectations that might be created by terms such as "parable," "instruction," or "sage." Heeding Kafka's implication that readers too not claim to fulfill such expectations, Benjamin's criticism performs that there is no accessible teaching on the basis of which Kafka must be read.

Such gesture of Benjamin and Kafka may be conceived as philosophic in so far as it avoids tragic identification of fate with a specific moral order. Plato often has Socrates emerge in defiance of any ostensibly seamless identification, in tragic myth, of moral order and fate (*O*, 113–14/I:1, 292–93). Admittedly, Plato's high regard for the "power of poetry" (*Macht der Dichtung*) also sometimes made him ban it from what he wanted to portray as the perfect community (*W* 2, 768/II:2, 683). The sole persistent basis of art— including poetry and literature—is, after all, the breakdown of any claim to perfect community. The latter claim, according to Benjamin, is tragic myth; it identifies fate with a specific moral-legal order. The antidote to such myth is *untragic* wisdom, which Benjamin detects in as wide array of presentations as Plato's *Phaedo*, medieval conceptions of Christ, the baroque mourning play, and Brecht's Galy Gay (e.g. *W* 4, 303–4/II:2, 533–34). Kafka too strikes Benjamin as a spoiler in relation to tragedy (II:3, 1263). If Kafka enters the tradition of untragic wisdom, however, he does so by celebrating no sage and by refusing to offer himself as one. If there is quasi-Taoist sagacity in Kafka's writings, it is sagacity without a sage (II:3, 1202, 1243, *W* 2, 813/II:2, 434–35). Brecht considers Kafka's "unlimited pessimism" to be "free from any tragic feeling of fate [*tragischen Schicksalsgefühl*]," and considers Kafka to be "wise" in responding with questions rather than with the heroics of the fascist's "indomitable iron will" (*W* 2, 787/VI, 529). The Kafka rendered by Benjamin, however, does not think he has wise questions. That might seem a variation of thinking one has wise answers. Indeed, much more than Brecht, Benjamin praises Kafka's reluctance to provide any counsel (786–88/528–30) and he translates *this* wisdom into the sparingly philosophic gesture of his reading of Kafka: a gesture of incompleteness that cannot credibly be overcome.

The historico-philosophic gesture of shame thus involves Kafka's "Ratlosigkeit" (II:3, 1207). In Kafka's works, there is "no longer any talk of wisdom." There are only "Zerfallsprodukte" of wisdom, only products of its disintegration (*W* 3, 326/*GB* 6, 112–3). The disintegration performs that it is impelled by what it cannot signify. In an early note, Benjamin identifies the temporary going-red, which may happen to some in shame, as a colour of "transience": a colour that comes and goes, is powerfully felt, yet leaves nothing to be understood and appears only as "[e]xpressionlessly signifying" (VI, 71). Kafka's parables—whether referred to as *Parabeln* or *Gleichnisse*— are similarly not parables strictly speaking, for there is nothing to teach; they are based above all on a "cloudy spot [*wolkige Stelle*]" (*W* 2, 802, 808 II:2, 420, 427; II:3, 1258, 1263).[27] It has been suggested above, however, that performance of disintegrating wisdom may indicate a wisdom of disintegration. The cloudy spot emerges as an opening against any societal guilt-context, an opening for shame about such guilt-contexts. The latter shame is an asceticism that inoculates against tragic myths of guilt-context. Such asceticism towards myth is the wisdom of the gesture of shame.[28]

In accordance with this asceticism, Benjamin follows the allure, the beauty, of Kafka's honesty that disclaims any epic counsel (*W* 2, 798/II:2, 413).[29] He considers the "misery" but also the "beauty" of Kafka's works to be that "they must be *more* than parables" (*W* 3, 326/*GB* VI, 113).[30] As suggested above, Kafka's gesture conveys symbol that is not contained by, and has an antinomic relationship with, any parabolic teaching-content (II:3, 1255). This gesture often becomes Benjamin's own in his accounts of Kafka-passages and of other authors' stories that he considers relevant to his discussion of Kafka.[31]

As implied already, the symbol emerges in a mystical gesture. Benjamin claims that he is developing a "mystical interpretation" of Kafka's writings—a mystical interpretation not of Kafka's "wisdom but of his foolishness" (II:3, 1172/*GB* 4, 526).[32] The dissociation from wisdom may be misleading, at least in light of Benjamin's aforementioned emphases on Kafka's historico-philosophic gesture and on Kafka's "Taoist" wisdom. Those emphases are compatible, however, with the mysticism that Benjamin seems to elicit from the foolishness of "the unfinished and the hapless" (*Unfertigen und Ungeschickten*), figures resonating with nature from which those not seeming fools have at least ostensibly separated themselves (*W* 2, 798–99/II:2, 414–15). The only release of such nature, the only help, comes in the form of the fool (*W* 3, 327/*GB* 6, 113).[33] Kafka's fools exist as reminders of our betrayal—in mythic attachments—of the nature that they indulge. Similarly, Robert Walser's protagonists illustrate the lack of a wish to "succeed." Such horror of success does not arise from "aversion before the world, moral ressentiment or pathos, but out of wholly Epicurean reasons." These figures "want to enjoy themselves" and they have an unusual ability to do so (*W* 2, 259/II:1, 327). In Walser's writings, as well as Kafka's, such twilight figures have no need to be more than that (*W* 2, 798/II:2, 414). In their gentle offence to our mythic attachments, these foolish figures become reminders of the transience and the contingency of those attachments. Rendering profane the attachments that we often treat as sacred, they perform pervasive mystery, and thereby register a mystical wisdom for Benjamin's reading.

Such wisdom necessitates, however, criticism not only of aspects of the Kafka-reception (such as the cheerful theologizing by Max Brod and others) but also of submissive aspects of Kafka's mysticism.[34] Kafka sometimes seems to Benjamin not far from Dostoyevsky's Grand Inquisitor, who concedes mystery that we do not understand, but considers this a justification for preaching subordination. Worrying about Kafka's possible interest in Rudolf Steiner's theosophy, Benjamin surmises: "Kafka did not always avoid the temptations of mysticism" (*W* 2, 804/II:2, 422).[35] Benjamin apparently does not consider these temptations to be constitutive or definitive of mysticism, for—as noted above—he proposes his own mystical interpretation. To some extent, his critique concerns the tendency of Kafka's mysticism to melt into the wish to be just an ordinary person. It also concerns the correlative tendency—in works such as *The Trial, The Castle,* and "Building the Chinese Wall"—to adopt a fatalistic relationship with organization (*W* 2, 803–4/II:2, 421–22). Kafka thus betrays the wisdom that is opened by his works—a wisdom for which no organizational form can credibly be considered fate.

Benjamin's criticism endeavours to extricate Kafka's wise shame from mythic tendencies in both Kafka's writings and the Kafka-reception. Trying in this way to intensify Kafka's gesture, Benjamin treats Kafka's historico-philosophic shame as anticipation of the continuance of the work in criticism.[36]

Inhumanly Tireless Astonishment

In a note of 1927 titled "Idea of a Mystery," Benjamin remarks that *mystery* is the sole complementarity of the various ways in which witness to mute nature, or the future, might credibly be given. The knowledge of the relevant philosophy (*W* 2, 68/II:3, 1153–54) can, it seems, only be communicated as ultimately incommunicable.[37] In the 1949-introduction to "What is Metaphysics?" however, Heidegger contends that metaphysics "remains the primary in philosophy" and that "the primary in thinking" is not reached by metaphysics.[38] In the wake of such remarks by Heidegger and Derrida, the risk of philosophy proclaiming too much for itself has led to distinctions of thinking from philosophy, which is then identified with a pathos—sometimes called the pathos of wonder. Thinking would avoid this pathos of metaphysical presumption to break with, and go beyond, nature. Such pathos belongs to a tradition of anthropomorphizing that ascribes human features or emotions to what is ultimately an unidentifiable dimension.[39] The shame in Benjamin's mystical philosophy could seem to indicate his participation in such a tradition of pathos.

Regarding shame, Benjamin takes his cue, of course, from Kafka. Most famously, K. in *The Trial* expresses shame at his own death by killers who represent the system that has judged him. K's shame seems a variation of what Benjamin's *Elective Affinities*-essay refers to as "inclination" (*Neigung*) that can bring hypostatized semblance to decline (*W* 1, 348–49/I:1, 191–92). Such inclination could be said to open to Nature itself.[40] The latter impels rejection of the betrayal of *physis* by humanly ascribed meaning.[41] In so far as Kafka's writings invoke such nature or *physis*, perhaps nowhere more pointedly than in the being-animal that gives Kafka a way to forgo "human form and human wisdom out of a kind of shame." Benjamin compares Kafka's being-animal with the way "a distinguished gentleman," who finds himself in a pub, "out of shame" dispenses with wiping out his glass (*W* 3, 327/*GB* VI, 113).[42] The being-animal is the recourse of someone ashamed of being-human. Admittedly, at the end of *The Trial*, K. complains that he dies "'[l]ike a dog!'" This does not, however, discredit the notion that K.'s shame at dying like a dog is shame of the human. Kafka writes "als sollte die Scham ihn überleben" (as though the shame was to outlive him),[43] but Agamben says with even greater confidence: "At the moment when the executioners' knives are about to penetrate his flesh, Joseph K. with one last leap succeeds in getting hold of the shame that will survive him."[44] K. might or might not reach the shame that will survive him. Agamben's confidence, conceivably influenced by Benjamin's (*W* 2, 808/II:2, 428), is perhaps partly based on confidence that the force impelling shame about sovereign power is inextinguishable. It is inhuman; it indulges no pathos, no anthropomorphic characterization. For Benjamin, this lack of indulgence, this shame, is just the insistence of thinking. Such shame is no more pathetic than is the invocation to think. Even the claim to think will be a pathetic fallacy if it is not always shamed into admitting that it is accompanied by, or involves, influences other than thinking itself. Only with such shame can thinking be thoughtful. Kafka's shame is simply the gesture of an inclination to think outside any parameters recognizably set by the myths that oppose this inclination. With this inclination, Kafka's "thinking itself has a gestural character" (II:3, 1238).

If Kafka is "tireless" (*unermüdlich*) in trying to register such gesture (*W* 2, 814/ II:2, 435–36), this follows from the inexhaustible boundlessness of the inhuman non-identifiable. Kafka's shame is distinct from "the tiresome astonishment" (*dem erschlaffenden Staunen*) of those who are astonished when confronted with the human suffering accompanying the societal myth to which they have become attached (*W* 1, 451/ IV:1, 95, and also see *W* 4, 392/1:2, 697).[45] Kafka's tireless effort at registering gesture involves "astonishment" (*Staunen*) (*W* 2, 814/II:2, 436), but this is a constant astonishment at human identifications. In relation to those identifications, Kafka tirelessly registers shame. This gesture of astonishment is the basis, therefore, of K.'s inability to adapt to human orders (814/435–36).[46]

Brecht, according to Benjamin, regards astonishment as Kafka's "theme": "Astonishment: The astonishment of a human being, who feels enormous shifts in all relations are in the offing, without being able himself to adapt to the new orders" (*W* 2, 477/II:3, 1203).[47] Concerning Brecht's epic theater, Benjamin refers to an astonishment that revives a Socratic praxis. This is a "hard and chaste" version of Socratic practice (*UB*, 4/II:2, 522). There is not supposed to be any pathos or anthropomorphism: "if the stream of things breaks against this rock of astonishment, then there is no difference between a human life and a word" (13/531). As Brecht breaks the human, the audience can "learn astonishment about the circumstances [*Zustände*] in which" the principal character "moves" (*W* 2, 304/II:2, 535). This could be considered astonishment about the production of human beings by myth. There is no pathos, for there is no identity—no Being—with which the astonishment is associating itself. The "Staunen" is without "Süffisance" (*UB*, 4, *W* 2, 778/II:2, 522, 698). This lack of complacency or satisfaction is all the more intense in Kafka, whose protagonists in the novels (Benjamin seems to mean *The Trial* and *The Castle*) do not rise above the "Ratlosigkeit" that they in no way want (II:3, 1221). The aforementioned Epicurean fools are also clueless and do not mind this for the most part, but they too are performances of a break with mythic counsel. The allure of the fools for us may be that they become possibilities for us to be astonished by our attachment to the myths deeming them fools.

If the astonishment may be conceived as a hard and chaste Socratic practice, an inhuman asceticism against myth, it involves no identitarian pathos but rather tireless shame about the pervasive identitarianism of myth. Such tireless shame is the basis for the continuation of Kafka's work in Benjamin's philosophic criticism.

ATTENTIVENESS

In various studies, Benjamin outlines this complementary relationship of art and philosophy. A service of philosophy to art works was mentioned early in this study: the persistence of discourse against any ostensibly concluded gesture of an art work. Such persistence continues the exercise—initiated by the art work—of breaking down myth. A further complementarity of art work and philosophy is that the art work's defiance of discursive rendering helps to keep philosophy philosophical. In the encounter with art works, philosophy is kept all the more attentive to the resistance of particularity to discursive rendering. Such unyielding is the philosophical element in the art work.[48] Attentiveness to this element of the art work is integral to the possibility of criticism being philosophy, love of wisdom.

Kafka's gesture impervious to myth is conveyed in Benjamin's remark that "the age in which Kafka lived" was considered by Kafka to be "no progress beyond the primal beginnings" (*keinen Fortschritt über die Uranfänge*). Kafka's writings juxtapose the latter creaturely dimension with the myth that denies or forgets it (*W* 2, 808–9/II:2, 428). For Kafka's historico-philosophical shame about myth, a sort of redemption may accordingly be the inexhaustible "past," which "presents itself as teaching [*die Lehre*], as wisdom [*die Weisheit*]" (II:3, 1205). Given Benjamin's aforementioned remarks that Kafka's works contain no teaching, it may be understood that *this* teaching, *this* wisdom, overwhelms; this past is no possession. It appears, and is recalled, solely as distortion that breaks down the would-be clarities of myth.

Kafka's literature is historico-philosophic, as is Benjamin's reading, in shame about the denial of distortion. The hunchbacked little man, the laughing "bucklicht Männlein," of a children's verse is considered by Benjamin to be emblematic of the "distortion" that pervades Kafka's writings. As such distortion, the *Vorwelt* intrudes as natural history that laughingly mocks the acclaimed clarity of our mythic attachments. In opening to distortion, in praying—as the child of the verse is beckoned to do—for the "bucklicht Männlein" too, there emerges what Benjamin refers to as Kafka's "attentiveness" (*Aufmerksamkeit*) for all creatures (*W* 2, 811/II:2, 432).[49] Kafka's attentiveness is unusually uncompromised by the disregard that is habit.[50]

Yet—according to Benjamin—the aforementioned prayers are to a Messiah whose coming would eliminate the distortions. The emblem of "distorted life," the "bucklicht Männlein" "will disappear if the Messiah comes." This will be the kind of "slight adjustment" that the Messiah would make (*W* 2, 811/II:2, 432).[51] Such remarks indicate a more patronizing attitude toward the "distortions," the *Vorwelt*, the lack of control, than is often evident in Benjamin's writings. In this respect, aspects of the Messianism in Benjamin's Kafka-writings could seem to betray the gesture of shame about myth, the shame that Benjamin otherwise presents as constitutive of Kafka's literature, and correlatively of his own account of that literature.

Although hardly from a Messianic standpoint, Axel Honneth has recently identified the autistic person and the amnesiac as pathological because they lack the normative that we—those in or with the normative—delegate.[52] As demonstrated in many of his explorations of literature and art, Benjamin's attentiveness to wayward singularity usually permits him to say nothing quite so brutal.[53] Indeed, much of what has been said above about his Kafka-writings has concerned a sensibility for which not only the *bucklicht Männlein* but also the autistic person and the amnesiac could conceivably become the historico-philosophic gesture that shames myth. Kafka's failures may have an allure, may be beautiful, precisely in shaming the myths that would deem something or someone a failure; if there is a gesture of shame in Kafka's literature, it performs a taking-exception to such myth. Literary freedom or licence is philosophic precisely in such ability to withstand—to take exception to—myth. Under the rubric of "exception," Philippe Sollers assembles and introduces a collection of some of his short pieces on works of literature and art: "Exception: telle est la règle en art et en littérature."[54]

The inexhaustible basis for taking exception, for shaming myth, could be a *messianicity* allied with literature, allied with literature in the latter's gesture of philosophic shame about myth.[55] This alliance with literature would be distinct from a Messianism that envisions ultimately overcoming the distortion or deviation explored by literature.[56]

The alliance with literature could not claim to know how history would end if a Messiah arrived. After all, Benjamin even claims that shame prevents Kafka in his writings from referring to God and from posing theological questions (II:3, 1207, 1210, 1212, 1213, 1237).

Literary attentiveness cannot, moreover, regard challenges to norms only as exceptions that corroborate the rule they offend; nor can it simply be a shift *from* exception and *to* allegedly responsible neighbourliness that would aim to eliminate—by slight adjustment—such exception.[57] The historico-philosophic gesture of shame echoes in Benjamin's suggestion—in "On the Concept of History"—that exception is the only permanent rule (*W* 4, 392/I:2, 697). For the relevant gesture, the autistic person, the amnesiac, the laughing hunchbacked little man, perform the limited reach, the failure, of answerability. Shame at myths of answerability, attentiveness to exception, can be more philosophic, more thoughtful, than is eagerly envisioning the elimination of exception by slight adjustment. Another way of putting this would be to say that the possibility of philosophy is diminished by the absence of literature.

"Literature" here pertains both to the literariness of philosophy—its gesture of inextinguishable silence—and to the exceptions that make literature a reminder of our distorted access to anyone and anything, including ourselves.

NOTES

I thank the three anonymous reviewers for their comments. Particularly the reviewers known to me as "one" and "three" provided comments that will be of relevance for future work.

1. Bernd Witte, *Der Intellektuelle als Kritiker. Untersuchungen zu seinem Frühwerk* (Stuttgart: J. B. Metzlersche Verlagsbuchhandlung, 1976), 5.
2. Theodor Adorno, *Über Walter Benjamin*, ed. R. Tiedemann, rev. ed. (Frankfurt/M.: Suhrkamp Verlag, 1990), 97–98. The suggestion that Benjamin was a poet and not a philosopher is made by Hannah Arendt, "Walter Benjamin: 1892–1940," trans. Harry Zohn, in *Men in Dark Times* (New York: Harcourt Brace Jovanovich, 1968), 166–67. On this topic, remarks by Adorno and Gershom Scholem in letters could also be noted: *Arendt und Benjamin: Texte, Briefe, Dokumente*, ed. Detlev Schöttker and Erdmut Wizisla (Frankfurt/M.: Suhrkamp, 2006), 181, 186. Benjamin did, of course, write poems and stories, but the debate between Arendt and Adorno concerns the writings usually regarded as exercises in philosophy and criticism.
3. Theodor Adorno, "Introduction to Benjamin's *Schriften*," trans. R. Hullot-Kentnor, in *On Walter Benjamin: Critical Essays and Recollections*, ed. Gary Smith (Cambridge, MA: MIT Press, 1988), 7/*Über Walter Benjamin*, 39.
4. See Theodor Adorno, *Negative Dialectics*, trans. E. B. Ashton (New York: Continuum, 1973), 53/*Negative Dialektik* (Frankfurt/M.: Suhrkamp, 1966), 62.
5. See Theodor Adorno and Walter Benjamin, *The Complete Correspondence 1928–1940*, trans. Nicholas Walker, ed. Henri Lonitz (Cambridge, MA: Harvard University Press, 1999), 66/II:3, 1173, 1174. Here and elsewhere, Roman numerals, sometimes followed by Arabic numerals, indicate volume numbers of Benjamin, *Gesammelte Schriften*, Vols. I–VII, ed. R. Tiedemann and H. Schweppenhäuser *et al.* (Frankfurt/M.: Suhrkamp Verlag 1974–99). The following abbreviations are also used for works by Benjamin: *C* = *The Correspondence of Walter Benjamin*, ed. Gershom Scholem and Theodor Adorno, trans. Manfred R. Jacobson and Evelyn M. Jacobson (Chicago, IL: University of Chicago Press, 1994); *GB* = *Gesammelte Briefe*, Vols. 1–6, ed. Christoph Gödde and Henri Lonitz (Frankfurt/M.: Suhrkamp Verlag,

1995–2000); $O =$ *The Origin of the German Tragic Drama*, trans. John Osborne (London: Verso, 1977); $UB =$ *Understanding Brecht*, trans. Anna Bostock (London: Verso, 1998); W (followed by a volume number) = *Selected Writings*, Vols. 1–4, ed. Michael W. Jennings *et al.* (Cambridge, MA: The Belknap Press of Harvard University Press, 1996, 1999, 2002, 2003). If an existing English-translation has been modified, the pagination for the German text will be italicized (*O*, 27/I:1, *207*).

6. Adorno and Benjamin, *The Complete Correspondence*, 69/II:3, 1176. The translation reads that these elements are "to be rendered dialectical through and through."

7. See Adorno in Adorno and Benjamin, *The Complete Correspondence*, 67–68/II:3, 1175. Benjamin provides a very conciliatory response to Adorno's early reservations (73–76/1178–79).

8. With regard to Benjamin's early writings, these points have more elaborate formulations in Monad Rrenban, *Wild, Unforgettable Philosophy in Early Works on Walter Benjamin* (Lanham, MD: Lexington Books, 2005), 59–119.

9. Giorgio Agamben, *Means without End: Notes on Politics*, trans. Vincenzo Binetti and Cesare Casarino (Minneapolis, MN: University of Minnesota Press, 2000), 56, 59–60. See too Agamben, "Notes on Gesture," in *Infancy and History: Essays on the Destruction of Experience*, trans. Liz Heron (London: Verso, 1993), 139; and Agamben, *Idea of Prose*, trans. Michael Sullivan and Sam Whitsitt (Albany, NY: State University of New York Press, 1995), 111.

10. For more on this aspect of Kafka and Chaplin, see II:3, 1257.

11. Also see notes in II:3, 1257, 1261.

12. Giorgio Agamben, *Idea of Prose*, 137–38.

13. Giorgio Agamben, "Kommerell, or On Gesture," in *Potentialities: Collected Essays in Philosophy*, trans. and ed. Daniel Heller-Roazen (Stanford, CA: Stanford University Press, 1999), 80.

14. *Ibid.*, 78–79.

15. Agamben, *Idea of Prose*, 85. The notion of shame developed in various books by Agamben is clearly influenced by Benjamin, although this is not made explicit. The most elaborate discussion of shame is *Remnants of Auschwitz: The Witness and the Archive*, trans. Daniel Heller-Roazen (New York: Zone Books, 2002), 26, 60, 87–135.

16. Agamben, "Kommerell, or On Gesture," 85. See too *Means without End*, 60.

17. See too II:3, 1214, 1261, 1267.

18. Points made in this paragraph, and relevant remarks by Franz Rosenzweig (as well as Werner Hamacher and Bernd Müller), are elaborated in a little more detail in an article that is scheduled to appear in early 2010.

19. In a very early note, Benjamin still writes the following. "Disgust and shame: relationship of these two affects [*Affekte*] and their significance in Kafka" (II:3, 1191).

20. See Werner Hamacher, *Premises: Essays on Philosophy and Literature from Kant to Celan*, trans. Peter Fenves (Stanford, CA: Stanford University Press, 1999), 294–336, and Samuel Weber, *Benjamin's-abilities* (Cambridge, MA: Harvard University Press, 2008), chaps. 7 and 13.

21. Gilles Deleuze and Félix Guattari, *What is Philosophy?*, trans. Janis Tomlinson and Graham Burchell III (New York: Columbia University Press, 1996), 107–8/ *Qu'est-ce que la philosophie?* (Paris: Les Éditions de Minuit, 1991), 103.

22. See Franz Kafka, *Der Verschollene*, ed. J. Schillemeit (Frankfurt/M.: Fischer, 2002), 387–417. For the relevant passage by Franz Rosenzweig, see his *The Star of Redemption*, trans. Barbara E. Galli (Notre Dame, IN: University of Notre Dame Press, 1985), 75/*Der Stern der Erlösung* (Frankfurt/M.: Suhrkamp, 1988), 81.

23. Also *W* 3, 326/*GB* VI, *112*; II:3, 1165, 1213, 1246.

24. Also II:3, 1220, 1244–45.

25. See too II:3, 1257, 1264.

26. See too II:3, 1259 and *W* 2, 784/VI, *525*.

27. An extensive discussion of the *cloudy spot* may be found in Hamacher, *Premises*, 298–308.

28. On such asceticism in Kafka's works, particularly the asceticism of study, see *W* 2, 813/II:2, 434–35. See too II:3, 1242.

29. See too II:3, 1216.
30. See too II:3, 1260 and the letter of January 7, 1935 to Adorno in *The Complete Correspondence*, 74/II:3, 1179.
31. See stories recounted in *W* 2, 794–95, 805–6, 812/II:2, 409–10, 424–25, 433 and II:3, 1255, 1260–61. For pertinent comments, see Rainer Nägele, "Die Aufmerksamkeit des Lesers," in *Enlightenments: Encounters between Critical Theory and Contemporary French Thought*, ed. H. de Vries and H. Kunneman (Kampen: Kok Pharos Publishing, 1993), 164–65.
32. See too *W* 3, 326–27/*GB* VI, 113.
33. For further remarks on fools, see II:3, 1212; *W* 2,798, 813, 816/II:2, 414, 434, 438.
34. Concerning Brod, see *C*, 595/*GB* VI, 220/II:3, 1183 and II:3, 1220, as well as *W* 3, 317–19/III, 526–29.
35. Also see II:3, 1257. For the relevant remarks of the Grand Inquisitor, see Fyodor Dostoevsky, *The Brothers Karamazov*, trans. Andrew H. MacAndrew (New York: Bantam Books, 1981), 309.
36. For extrapolation of this notion of criticism in the art work and as continuance of the art work, see Rrenban (166–69) with regard to earlier works by Benjamin. For a later, "materialist" formulation, see Benjamin's comment of around 1931 that "criticism is internal [*innerlich*] to the work" (*W* 2, 547/VI, 172).
37. The note accompanies a letter that ends with the sentence: "Als Krankenengel habe ich an meinem Lager Kafka. Ich lese den 'Prozeß'" [II:3, 1154/*GB* III, 303]).
38. Martin Heidegger, "Introduction to 'What is Metaphysics?,'" trans. Walter Kaufmann and William McNeill, in *Pathways*, ed. and trans. William McNeill (Cambridge: Cambridge University Press, 1998), 279/*Wegmarken*, *Gesamtausgabe* Vol. 9 (Frankfurt/M.: Vittorio Klostermann, 1976), *367*. See too: 280–82/368–72.
39. Rodolphe Gasché, *The Honor of Thinking: Critique, Theory, Philosophy* (Stanford, CA: Stanford University Press, 2007), 348, 350–55, 360.
40. For the formulation "Nature itself," see Gilles Deleuze and Félix Guattari, *Kafka: Toward a Minor Literature*, trans. D. Polan (Minneapolis, MN: University of Minnesota, 1986), 35/*Kafka. Pour une Littérature Mineure* (Paris: Les Éditions de Minuit, 1975), 64.
41. On this betrayal, see *O*, 226/I:1, 400.
42. See too II:3, 1261–62 and *C*, 453/*GB* IV, 478/II:3, 1165.
43. Franz Kafka, *The Trial*, trans. Breon Mitchell (New York: Schocken Books, 1999), 231/*Der Proceß*, ed. M. Palsey, *Kritische Ausgabe* (Frankfurt/M.: Fischer, 2002), *312*.
44. Agamben, *Means without End*, 132–33. See too *Remnants*, 104.
45. It seems mistaken, therefore, to suggest—as many do (e.g. Weber, *Benjamin's-abilities*, 107, 335 n. 17) that the amazement or astonishment mentioned in such passages is the same as the astonishment or amazement discussed in Benjamin's writings on Brecht or Kafka.
46. See too II:3, 1204–5.
47. For elaboration, see *W* 2, 477–79/II:3, 1203–5 and *W* 2, 496/II:2, 678.
48. This relationship of philosophy and art has a very careful formulation in the *Elective Affinities*-study (*W* 1, 333–34/I:1, 172–73). Such formulations seem incompatible with the suggestion of Andrew Benjamin that Benjamin has no notion of "literature" as "inherently philosophical" (*Philosophy's Literature* [Manchester: Clinamen, 2001], 19).
49. See too *W* 3, 384–85/IV:1, 302–3/VII:1, 429–30/*Berliner Kindheit um neunzehnhundert (Gießener Fassung)* (Frankfurt/M.: Suhrkamp, 2000), 109–11. For the verse "Das buckliche Männlein," see "Kinderlieder" in *Des Knaben Wunderhorn. Alte deutsche Lieder*, Vol. 3, ed. L. Achim von Arnim and Clemens Brentano (Heidelberg: Mohr und Zimmer, 1808), 54–55. Benjamin cites as his source, however, Georg Scherer's *Das Deutsche Kinderbuch* (*W* 3, 385/IV:1, 303/VII:1, 430/*Gießener Fassung*, 109).
50. For comments on habit and attentiveness, see *W* 2, 592/IV:1, 407–8.
51. Benjamin quotes "a great rabbi." It has been claimed that this "rabbi" is Scholem (Young-Ok Kim, *Selbstporträt im Text des Anderen. Walter Benjamins Kafka-Lektüre* [Frankfurt/M.: Peter Lang, 1995], 71 n. 106). The claim seems to be based on Ernst Bloch's reference to a similar

dictum, which Bloch ascribes to "a really Kabbalistic" rabbi (*Spuren* [Frankfurt/M.: Suhrkamp, 1983 (first edition, 1930)], 201–2).

52. Axel Honneth, *Verdinglichung. Eine anerkennungstheoretische Studie* (Frankfurt/M.: Suhrkamp, 2005), 48–51, 70.

53. It could be debated, however, whether Benjamin's account of Kurt Goldstein's analysis of aphasia (*W* 3, 85–86/III, 480) does not somewhat resemble Honneth's portrayals of the autistic person and the amnesiac. More "literary" is Benjamin's commentary on hysteria and on the idiot in Dostoyevsky's *The Idiot* (*W* 1, 80/II:1, 240).

54. Philippe Sollers, *Théorie des Exceptions* (Paris: Gallimard, 1986), 11.

55. Although the context for Derrida's usage of the term "messianicity" is quite different from what is developed here, there could be a relevance here of his notion of "messianicity without messianism," a messianicity that would be an "opening to the future . . . but without horizon of expectation and without prophetic prefiguration." Jacques Derrida, "Faith and Knowledge," trans. Samuel Weber, in *Acts of Religion*, ed. Gil Anidjar (New York: Routledge, 2002), 56. Less than Derrida do I note this notion of messianicity as an objection to all Messianism. Nor do I wish to object to all of Benjamin's Messianism. I am trying only to highlight some concerns that could arise with regard to the Messianism in Benjamin's writing on Kafka.

56. In contrast, Eric L. Santner favours those elements of Benjamin's Messianism that present a counterforce to the creaturely, the *Vorwelt*. Eric L. Santner, *On Creaturely Life: Rilke, Benjamin, Sebald* (Chicago, IL: University of Chicago Press, 2006), 24–25, 92–95, 130–31.

57. This differs with Eric Santner, "Miracles Happen: Benjamin, Rosenzweig, Freud, and the Matter of the Neighbor," in *The Neighbor: Three Inquiries in Political Theology*, ed. Slavoj Žižek, Eric L. Santner, and Kenneth Reinhard (Chicago, IL: University of Chicago Press, 2005), 99–100, 130–31.

Stanley Cavell and Two Pictures of the Voice

~ Adam Gonya ~

ABSTRACT *In the way we traffic with words we might distinguish between deliberate conceptual performances—knowing more or less what we want to say and finding the right words for it—and others in which the conscious mind is more receptive. If a philosophical text is a deliberate compilation of words, then what is the philosopher to make of this second, non-deliberate sort of conceptual performance? Each "picture of the voice" is elaborated, the first in the work of Schopenhauer, the second in Nietzsche. A similar distinction is explored in the theoretical work of the poet Seamus Heaney. This leads to consideration of how two of Stanley Cavell's more important mentors, Wittgenstein and Emerson, have responded to Shakespeare. Their differing appraisals, I hope to show, depend upon their affinities with one of these two pictures. My conclusion briefly suggests how this contrast illuminates the work of Stanley Cavell.*

Suppose we are writing a text. Knowing more or less what we want to get across, we deliberately select the words that express our meaning. We might say that in this case our intellect, our conscious mind, is doing the work. But at other times it seems the intellect is merely receiving. Not chosen in light of some idea, it seems the words *themselves* become active. Some interplay between these two seems to be present when, in the *Philosophical Investigations*, Wittgenstein asks:

> What happens when we make an effort—say in writing a letter—to find the right expression for our thoughts?—This phrase compares the process to one of translating or describing: the thoughts are already there (perhaps they were in advance) and we merely look for their expression.... But mayn't all sorts of things happen here? I surrender to a mood and the expression *comes*.[1]

Part of being a writer, then, would involve developing a productive calibration between the two ends of this spectrum—these two ways of relating to language—now selecting the word we mean, now receiving the word that *comes*. Though temperament might incline us more to one way than another, for novelists or poets, or indeed almost anyone working with language, in principle it hardly matters which predominates, so long as we get the words we want on the page.

~

But is it the same for the philosopher? Whatever else it may be, a philosophical text typically presents itself as a deliberate and considered compilation of words. And if it is deliberate, then *behind* every word—every clause, every preposition—there is, so goes the assumption, the clear and distinct thought, a claim of responsibility for just these implications. What is the philosopher to make of the words that, rather than being deliberately selected by the intellect, simply *come*? Is it wise for the philosopher to trust this energy? Might it not conceal meanings, stowaways of the unintended? Quite apart from his or her own temperamental inclinations, then, the philosopher may also have occupational qualms concerning what we might call the energies of occurrence.

This article explores how these two ways of trafficking in words have found philosophical elaboration in the work of Schopenhauer, Nietzsche, and Stanley Cavell. All three are concerned with the self's relation to intelligibility. Yet each gives a different picture of how these two ways—the assertive and the receptive—interact in making the self intelligible. And this, in turn, depends on the region of the self from which the words originate, what we are calling the *voice*. Part 1 takes Schopenhauer as an exemplar of the first picture of the voice, where we make ourselves intelligible through deliberate intellectual assertion upon language in the service of an idea. In this case, the intellect is the seat of the voice. From Nietzsche we get the second picture. Rather than assertion, Nietzsche's account endorses the non-deliberate energies of occurrence from outside the ambit of the intellect. Part 2 touches on correspondences in a pair of lectures by the poet Seamus Heaney, who offers what I take to be a parallel distinction in the craft of poetry. This leads, in the third part, to consideration of how two of Stanley Cavell's more important mentors, Wittgenstein and Emerson, have responded to Shakespeare. Their differing appraisals, I hope to show, depend upon their affinities with one of these two pictures. I conclude that Cavell's work may be read to suggest that attempts to close down the second route—to overcome the energy of occurrence with the energy of assertion—precariously strain our ability to make ourselves intelligible.

1. Schopenhauer is sometimes presented as a philosopher of the irrational, and certainly with good reason. After all, the will—which in his philosophy is quite literally everything—is not in the least bit rational. But then whatever *we* are, each of us, as individuated conscious beings, is by the same token intimately bound up with our rational capacities. And for Schopenhauer the only job of the intellect is to *perceive*.

> As from the direct light of the sun [he writes] to the borrowed reflected light of the moon, so do we pass from the immediate representation of perception, which stands by itself and is its own warrant, to reflection, to the abstract, discursive concepts of reason [*Vernuft*], which have their whole content only from that knowledge of perception, and in relation to it.[2]

The problem is that the will is constantly blocking our attempts to perceive existence under our own power. So deceptively has the will contrived things that we perceive only in accordance with its interests. In everyday life, then, in everything we look at, in everything we do, we are alienated from our nature as a perceiving intellect.

But there are moments when we do manage to break loose. Brimming with an inborn power to see things as they *are*, the intellect escapes the surveillance of the will and becomes, at last, what Schopenhauer calls the pure knowing subject. Such a subject glimpses what are called the (Platonic) Ideas, the modes into which the singular will, the thing-in-itself, shatters as it enters the realm of representation. These moments are intense, heartening, but desperately short. And when they cease, the genius is returned to the suffering and ignorance of empirical consciousness, no longer a pure knowing subject, but a willing subject, once again an alienated drone. After awhile the genius basically gets sick of this. Rather than trying to perceive the Ideas—only, once again, to be dragged back down into the pain of empirical consciousness—he seeks instead to quiet the will within himself.

Before any of that, however, the genius has another problem. As we have seen, perception is the gold standard. But how can anything perceived during our epiphanies come to be expressed? Concepts are not just feeble abstractions from this perception—they are formed in fealty to the pressures of empirical consciousness.

> Words and *concepts* [he writes] will always be *barren and dry*, for this is their nature . . . .
> The thought itself is only the mummy of . . . perception and the words are the lid of the
> sarcophagus. Here we have the limit of mental communication; it excludes the best.[3]

If we fail to speak from pure perception, we are merely repeating shallow abstractions. But since the pure knowing subject glimpses truths outside the realm of empirical consciousness, *no words could possibly describe them.*

What does the Schopenhauerian poet do? Having perceived the Ideas, the poet *then* takes language into his workshop and artfully combines concepts so that they mutually limit their otherwise sterile abstractions.[4] The poet is like a chemist "who obtains solid precipitates by combining perfectly clear and transparent fluids" (*WWR* I, 243). Only as intellectual signs, then, do words have any power to reveal the Ideas. Formal aspects, if they add anything, merely add pleasure. In fact the empirical qualities of words—their sound, texture, rhythm, etc.—often imperil the poet's attempt to express the content of perception.[5] Even the expert poet can only take partial credit for a poem: "Thus he [the poet] is only half responsible for all that he says; meter and rhyme must answer for the other half" (*WWR* II, 427). Language could just as readily endorse shallowness, so that "even distorted and false ideas gain an appearance of truth through versification" (*WWR* II, 429). If the poems of great artists give the impression of being discovered in language, this is a delightful but hard-won illusion, the result of the genius managing to work this heterogeneous material, grooved with its alien grain.

For Schopenhauer, the "correct and pure expression" of an idea should be in prose, which he appears to hold as a kind of expressive benchmark.

> Even famous passages from famous poets [he writes] shrink up again and become
> insignificant when they are faithfully reproduced in prose. If only the true is beautiful,
> and the most cherished adornment of truth is nakedness, then an idea [*Gedanke*] which
> appears great and beautiful in prose will have more true worth than one that has the
> same effect in verse. It is very surprising and well worth investigation that such trifling,
> and indeed apparently childish, means as metre and rhyme produce so powerful an
> effect. (*WWR* II, 429)

There is much one might want to say to this, especially to the notion that poetry could somehow be *faithfully* reproduced in prose—how, for one thing, could we devise a standard of fidelity? But let us now try to summarize this first picture of the voice. Three points deserve emphasis: (1) The knowing intellect is the seat of the voice, i.e., the origin of our words; (2) To express the content of perception, the poet *works* on language, the recalcitrant medium of empirical consciousness; and (3) No new aspects are discovered in expression; expression is a move away from the perception's original purity, an exile among alien aspects.

Nietzsche provides us with the second picture of the voice, which by contrast endorses the energies of occurrence. In *The Birth of Tragedy* the origin of our words is not the intellect; it is the "musical mood."[6] Under the influence of a musical mood, the poet *senses* the presence of an intuition, but the poet has no direct intellectual *access*. Though the musical mood is *within* consciousness, it remains closed to consciousness. Though closed, it asserts its own expressive exigency upon the materials of intellectual exchange, and emerges as what is called the "poetic idea." Schopenhauer's pure knowing subject *purifies* itself to perceive the Ideas. In Nietzsche's picture, however, the insights, powered by alien enthusiasm, *contaminate* themselves, taint and pollute themselves with the impurities of our everyday conceptual forms, while never allowing these forms to become windows into their interiors. As intellectual signs, they are meaningless. Rather than explain and lay bare, conceptual forms cling to them haphazardly. These and all the formal aspects Schopenhauer's poet failed to master are now sported with the happy indifference of a God in terrestrial disguise.

I have said this energy is *alien* to the intellect: what does that mean? First, the energy is alien because it works along a precisely contrary tangent. The intellect seeks abstraction—the inference from specificity to generality. Nowhere is this better exemplified than in Schopenhauer. In fact you could argue that Schopenhauer's intimacy with the world amounted to a doomed fantasy of intellectual union, an unobstructed continuation along that very tangent of abstraction to nothing less than the ultimate condition, the unitary will. *The Birth of Tragedy*, however, has this reversed. Not the story of particularity coming under ultimate singularity, but rather this very singularity shattering into multiplicity: *that* is the tangent that interests Nietzsche. And it is only when the innate operation of the intellect breaks down that these other energies come to expression. Dionysian rapture (*Rausch*) amounts to the "breaking asunder of the individual and its becoming one with the primal being itself" (*BT*, 44). This is the condition for genuine creativity. Unhindered by the petty exertions of the intellect, the enthusiasts become "a medium, the channel through which the one truly existing subject celebrates its release and redemption in semblance" (*BT*, 32). Rather than an (intellectual) energy that would subsume, Nietzsche's Dionysian energy craves expansiveness, yearns to transcend itself in "explosive unity."[7] Not the unity of gathering, but rather the unity of squander, of capriciously variegated self-discovery. This is why these Dionysian insights *force* themselves upon us, disdaining any fixed, determinate form.

But how does the voice—the musical mood as origin—find expression in language? Before these Dionysian insights can come into contact with the Apollonian, there is an intervening step; here the reference to music is relevant. Music acts as a sort of mid–point between the conscious mind and the primordial unity. According to Schopenhauer, any sympathetic God who descended to reveal all the secrets of the universe would, to our earthly ears, proclaim at best in a booming gibberish (*WWR* II, 185).[8] But now what if this God had sung? And indeed this is what, out of its own inborn urge to luxuriate in diversity, the primal being consents to do. Only *into* music can the unity (*das Ur-Eine*) discharge what cannot possibly *ever* be spoken. The lyric poet, as a Dionysian artist, "entirely at one with the primordial unity . . . produces a copy of this primordial unity as music" (*BT*, 30). As a Dionysian he can go no further, but now, "under the influence of Apolline dream, the music becomes visible to him as in a *symbolic dream-image*."

So what can we say about this second picture of voice? (1) Not the (knowing) intellect but rather the *musical mood* is origin of our words; (2) Language is not a recalcitrant medium. In the discharge of a musical mood, all properties of language are solicited—these being the empirical aspects of language the Schopenhauerian poet could never quite subdue. And yet the poem is still only a trace; the intellect cannot recuperate the content of the musical mood through interpretation; and (3) Expression implies a discovery in new aspects. Neither diminished nor alienated, in expression the voice now *discovers* itself anew in the poet's words, its newfound lovely semblance. This is not a Schopenhauerian exile; this is an escape from an inhospitable homeland.

2. Consider a similar contrast in the theoretical work of the poet Seamus Heaney. He distinguishes between two sorts of conceptual performance in response to the triggering impulse. First the impulse: "It is my impression that this haunting or *donné* occurs to all poets in much the same way, arbitrarily, with a sense of promise, as an alertness, a hankering, a readiness." We might recognize this as the musical mood, that mysterious intimation of the poem in *potential*. Like Nietzsche's, Heaney's image is explicitly musical: he calls it the "tuning fork". Heaney goes on: "It is also my impression that the quality of the music in the finished poem has to do with the way the poet proceeds to respond to his *donné*."[9]

Two ways of responding seem to correspond to the two pictures just described. Heaney distinguishes between the masculine and feminine actions. Consider first the feminine, which would seem allied to Nietzsche's model. No less a poet than Shakespeare serves as an example. In *Timon of Athens*, the Poet says:

> A thing slipp'd idly from me.
> Our poesy is as a gum which oozes
> From whence 'tis nourished: the fire i' the flint
> Shows not till it be struck; our gentle flame
> Provokes itself, and, like the current, flies
> Each bound it chafes.[10]

You might see this as a Shakespearian account of how the poet ought to comport himself toward his musical mood. Whatever is giving itself language here discovers no stability, no finality, in any single image, but plows through several: a thing that slipped, an oozing "gum"; a spark-throwing flint; a "gentle flame"; a current. To anyone of a different temperament—and Nietzsche's Socrates comes to mind—this is a series of nonsensical contradictions.[11] Because how does it, this poet's *thing*, sustain itself through *gum* to *flames* to *water*? The Dionysian tangent, as we have seen, disdains any fixed expression.

According to Heaney, this is "a vision of poetic creation as a feminine action, almost parthenogenetic," meaning self-generating, self-triggering, like the self-provoking flame. "And out of this vision of feminine action comes a language for poetry that tends to brood and breed, crop and cluster, with a texture of echo and implication, trawling the pool of the ear with a net of associations."[12]

The masculine action, on the other hand, seeks "to master rather than to mesmerize the ear,"[13] "not complaisance but control" (71), a response that appears more in line with Schopenhauer's assertive picture. To the impulse, to the inceptive musical mood, the masculine rejoinder is not to surrender, but to force it into the daylight of assertion. "[T]he origin of [masculine] poetry [is] not a sinking but a coming up against . . . not an alluring but an alerting strain" (72). The response to the mood is not freely flowing, but pertinaciously "hammered into a unity" (75). The words, Heaney writes, "are crafted together more than they are coaxed out of one another, and they are crafted in the service of an idea that precedes the poem" (84). Language in the masculine mode is based on "assertion or command, and the poetic effort has to do with the conscious quelling and control of the materials, a labour of shaping; words are not music before they are anything else, nor are they drowsy from their slumber in the unconscious, but athletic, capable, displaying the muscle of sense"(88).

Let the poet and playwright Ben Jonson serve as a characteristic masculine poet. Though he admired Shakespeare, he also criticized his friend's fluency. "I remember the players have often mentioned it as an honour to Shakespeare that in his writing, whatsoever he penned, he never blotted a line. My answer hath been, 'Would he had blotted a thousand . . . . He flowed with the facility that sometime it was necessary he should be stopped.'"[14]

Heaney relates the music of the poem to the way poets respond to their *donné*. But the suggestion now is to see behind the masculine and feminine actions the two pictures of the voice, each with their interests and aspirations for what ought to happen in the conceptual performance. Along the axis of *intelligibility*, the masculine seeks to *discipline* the expressive impetus according to its interests, like the Schopenhauerian poet, who knows the Ideas and takes language into his workshop to overcome its inborn recalcitrance. Along the axis of *self-revelation*, the feminine instead *surrenders* to the impetus, like the Nietzschean poet, in whose words the musical mood discharges its mysterious burden without the surveillance of the conscious mind. The first is suspicious of how words can *surge*, smuggling in their alien aspects. But the second rides this energy eagerly, this "original generating rhythm,"[15] welcoming the new aspects in its conceptual costume—its newfound lovely semblance.

3. Ben Jonson is not the only one with reservations about Shakespeare. According to Stanley Cavell, in his recent essay, "The Interminable Shakespearian Text," Wittgenstein could only admire Shakespeare with reluctance. What hesitations did Wittgenstein have about Shakespeare? As we have seen in the quotation from *Timon of Athens*—though others could easily be found—the images, even the syntax, seem merely indications of a presence which disdains the sort of clean, naked encapsulation that Schopenhauer, for one, required as a condition of poetic truth. Wittgenstein meanwhile placed great emphasis on bringing "language back home, back to the order he calls the ordinary,

of calling language to attention, retrieving it, as if anew, from chaos."[16] So it might make sense, as Cavell has pointed out, that Shakespeare would cause him unease. "The reason I cannot understand Shakespeare," Wittgenstein writes, "is that I want to find symmetry in all this asymmetry . . . . His pieces give me an impression as of enormous sketches . . . as though they had been dashed off by someone who can permit himself *anything* so to speak" (48). Ben Jonson would have agreed. Someone who surrenders to his facility— which should rather be resisted, harnessed, hammered—will not produce finished works but instead "enormous sketches." Someone who allows himself *anything* will not even bother to blot out a line, if the report of the players is to be believed. Shakespeare's words, Cavell infers, lack "a certain *finish*" which makes Wittgenstein wonder at their real worth—it is a finish that amounts to "the momentary breaking off of a stretch of language from the rest of what is being said." And it is this finish, Cavell goes on,

> that Wittgenstein misses in Shakespeare's effects of, let's say, the maelstrom of significance. The matter is of such interest to me that I mark it for further study by hazarding further the thought, put more positively, that what Wittgenstein senses in Shakespeare's language is the continuous threat of chaos clinging to his creation, an anxiety produced as the sense that it is something miraculous that words can mean at all, that such things can be said, that there are words. This suggests another approach to Wittgenstein's, hence positivism's, obsession with the possibility of meaninglessness, which they liked to call, in different tones, nonsense. (49)

Wittgenstein's demand for finish: is *this* what Jonson thought Shakespeare would gain from blotting a thousand lines? *Finish* evidently contrasts with, is imperiled by, Shakespeare's overindulged *facility*, producing what Cavell calls the "maelstrom of significance." The more you surrender to facility, the less the finish, the more chaos threatens. Which means, seen now explicitly from the point of view of the masculine action: the less deliberate crafting and mastering that goes on, the less that meaning is really yours, broken off, set apart, secured against nonsense. *Our* meaning in this picture is under constant threat. If we mean anything it is because we overcome the chaotic energies of language always threatening to dissipate what we are trying to assert. *Finish*, you might say, acts like a semantic sealant.

But what about the second picture of the voice? Cavell compares Wittgenstein's response with Emerson's appraisal of Shakespeare, which might, at first, seem rather simplistic. "Shakespeare's principal merit," Emerson writes, "may be conveyed in saying that he of all men best understands the English language, and can say what he will." Cavell goes on to clarify:

> But this observation takes on life read against Wittgenstein's responses. Emerson's denial of originality seems remote from Wittgenstein's claim of uniqueness . . . . Noting that Wittgenstein's responses all have to do with his relation to Shakespeare's language quite generally—as not liking it, as looking for a finish that it negates, as wanting to admire it but put off by others' praises of it—Emerson's praise serves to complete the thought that our relation to Shakespeare is the model or test of our relation to language as such. (50)

Shakespeare's genius is unoriginal because he represents the flourishing of a capacity that lies in each of us. In that sense, says Emerson, "the greatest genius is the most indebted man" (49). He can sometimes be *us* more than we manage to be ourselves. The rare feat of genius is to "say what he will" and give exemplary voice to the "otherness of genius in each of us" (51). Shakespeare fulfills, in magisterial dimensions, the burdensome, indeed unrelenting imperative of human expression: that of making the self intelligible. This is too much for someone like the common man, whose "every word chagrins us." Why? Not because his words are unintelligible exactly. Everyone understands what he says. But his words afford, as it were, no opening into which *his* voice may pass—to adopt an image of Emerson's, in which God has his own secret passage into each of us, like an Emperor into his theater. This is why in rebuking him we do not know where to start. What is needed is not a different word here or there, but, *underneath*, an entirely different sort of relationship to language.

And this is where Shakespeare is especially valuable. A genius like Shakespeare, says Emerson, liberates in four ways. He emancipates us from our ego, from the fashions of the times, from idolatry, and from melancholy. "Now melancholy," Cavell goes on, "idolatry, entrapment in the views of others, and blindness to the existence of others trace a profile of skepticism. How are we to understand language, or what I was calling our relation to language, to liberate us from this complex?" Emerson attributes this to Shakespeare's demonstration, for the first time,

> [of] "the possibility of the translation of things into song." This is a figure Emerson uses both for what he calls in one paragraph "the powers of expression," and for what he calls in the next paragraph "perfect representation, at last." In the former he speaks of "transferring the inmost truth of things into music or verse" as "add[ing] a new problem to metaphysics," and in the latter he compares its addition, this breakthrough to the discovery of the source of song, with a technical breakthrough of the era: "Daguerre learned how to let one flower etch its image on his plate of iodine, and then proceeds at leisure to etch a million." (51)

In a lengthy parenthetical remark in *The Claim of Reason*, Cavell distinguishes between the *economy* of speech and the *aesthetics* of speech.[17] This in a more recent work he glosses by saying: "the former refer[s] to the control of concepts by criteria, the latter to the revelations of myself by what I find worth saying, or not saying, as and when I speak, or hold my tongue."[18] I associate what we have been calling the two pictures of the voice with these two parts of speech. In other words, the *economy* of the speech accounts for the interests of the first picture of the voice (intelligibility as such), while the *aesthetics* of speech account more for the interests of the second (self-revelation). Each conceptual performance, then, as we go on, binds together the two sets of interests and aspirations.

Wittgenstein seems more interested in the *economy of speech*, how criteria govern concepts, how intelligibility is maintained.[19] From this point of view, language is continually threatened by nonsense, of people pulling away from our shared criteria and forms of life. But Emerson seems more concerned with the *aesthetics of speech*, with self-revelation. And so Emerson might say (as might (Cavell's) Thoreau and Kierkegaard): grant that we have established these forms of life, or criteria, or conditions of meaning— well so what? Only *you* can sense if you have really spoken, because only you have access to the intimation, the premonition, the secret stirrings of your words, call it the musical mood, call it whatever you like, which you seek to discover in expression. What good if my words are objectively meaningful, shielded by finish from the hiss of nonsense, if they are not *my* words? What good if I am unable to discover an intimacy with them, even though they may be perfectly understandable? This is the Emersonian nightmare: a world in which slabs are fetched, apples purchased, children reproved, parents rebuked, speeches given, and ballots cast—but where no one, incredibly, actually *means* a word they say. And though they may never cease holding forth, they live, as Thoreau would call it, lives of "quiet desperation," or in the words of Emerson, "silent melancholy."[20] So the perpetual crisis in our lives as expressive beings is not the threat of nonsense. It is what Emerson calls *conformity*.

4. Cavell's point is that both parts of speech are necessary, the economy of speech (control of concepts by criteria) and the aesthetics of speech (self-revelation). Intelligibility might be seen as a matter of these two interests coming into some sort of productive calibration. But if each has different interests, then they can easily fall into contention. This is the relevance of the skeptic.

Possessed of an "illimitable desire,"[21] the skeptic demands an immediate intellectual connection to the world and the self, but also to the origin of his or her words. The skeptic aspires to relate to language solely according to the first picture of the voice. Ordinary language becomes disappointing—because where, after all, do *those* words come from? They have to be called, *summoned* by first asking the question: *what we say when*. Musical moods, or indeed any sort of intimation closed to the intellect, become an intolerable blockage. Hence skepticism is "an argument of the self with itself (over its finitude)."[22] At the end of the skeptical recital, if it ever really ends, the skeptic is left speaking from a position of emptiness, alienated and unintelligible. The failure of the skeptic marks what Cavell calls the truth of skepticism: that "the human creature's basis in the world as a whole, its relation to the world as such, is not that of knowing, anyway not what we think of as knowing."[23]

What the skeptic needs is therapy, which, keeping to this context, means learning to relate differently to expressive potencies outside the intellect—the province of the second picture of the voice. "The quest of this book," Cavell writes of Thoreau's *Walden*, "is for the recovery of the self, as from an illness."[24] Thoreau enjoins us to reinterpret the intellect's relation to the rest of the self, not as a limitation, but as neighboring, as being beside ourselves in a sane sense. Not by binding refractory parts together, nor by annexing one to the other, but by easing them into relation across a remove of difference and allowing, with trust rather than suspicion, that there *be* this distance between words and origin. This is how we recover a salutary wholeness of self; how we return life to our language.

> We are [Cavell writes] to reinterpret our sense of doubleness as a relation between ourselves in the aspect of indweller, unconsciously building, and in the aspect of a spectator, impartially observing. Unity between these aspects is not viewed as a mutual absorption, but as a perpetual nextness, an act of neighbouring or befriending.[25]

Cavell also hears Emerson insisting on the need to reinterpret this relation. Through the clutching of our concepts we lose the world. Emerson writes: "I take this evanescence and lubricity of all objects, which lets them slip through our fingers when we clutch hardest, to be the most unhandsome part of our condition."[26] Instead of putting the world together—instead of it hinging upon our faculties, us *knowing* it—we receive it. "Our relation to [the world's] existence is deeper—one which is accepted, that is to say, received."[27] We receive, for instance, our genius—but only if we learn to receive it from a distance, from an origin, you might say, closed to intellectual inspection. What is required is self-reliance, resolve, an enacting of our existence, usually without any warrant aside from the mere fact that this intimation is mine. "The call of one's genius," Cavell writes, "presents itself with no deeper authority than whim. And what presents itself in the form of whim is bound sometimes to be exactly whim and nothing more."[28] For both Thoreau and Emerson the energy of occurrence is decisive. The writer's calling, Thoreau suggests, "depends on his letting words come to him from their own regions."[29] And the poet, Emerson writes, enjoys a relation to language in which "in every word he speaks he rides on them as the horses of thought." Cavell comments: "The idea is that the words have a life of their own over which our mastery is the other face of our obedience."[30]

Making the self intelligible—not just *speaking* intelligibly, but giving expression to the *self*—requires resources both within the intellect (where the intellect is assertive and deliberate), and from outside (where the intellect is passive and receptive). How these two are brought into collaboration describes your comportment toward the perpetual *donné* of your life.

But what about the philosopher? Unevenly distributed on either side of the philosophical divide (between "analytical" and "continental" philosophy), there are, Cavell surmises, two pictures of how language relates to the world.

> One between those in either space whose intuition of the issue of language and the world is that language comes to be hooked onto or emitted into the world, and one between those whose intuition is, with some perhaps necessary vagueness, of a reverse direction, in which the world calls for words, an intuition that words are, I will say, world-bound, that the world, to be experienced, is to be answered, that this is what words are for.[31]

Cavell is temperamentally more in accord with this second picture, in which words are "world-bound." In this connection Cavell quotes Wittgenstein: "My relation to my words [that is, to my utterances] is wholly different from other people's." But if our words are not prepared at some metaphysical register before expression, what is our relation to our own voice? Where do our words come from? In response Cavell asks: "What is it to hear music?" "What is it to hear music's origin, hear it originating, what the composer hears?"[32] Of course a philosopher writing from a musical origin—would this be a music-making Socrates?—is liable to produce work which, to some ears at least, will be of questionable philosophical seriousness. And yet according to what we have seen of this second picture of the voice, a musical origin would aspire to contrast the traditional philosopher's clarity not with obscurity, but instead with the sort of incandescent precision in which, for instance, Shakespeare's *Othello* illuminates our lives with skepticism. But then we have to ask:

> Can philosophy accept [Othello and Desdemona] back at the hands of poetry? Certainly not as long as philosophy continues, as it has from the first, to demand the banishment of poetry from its republic. Perhaps it could if it could itself become literature. But can philosophy become literature and still know itself?[33]

NOTES

An earlier version of this article was presented in 2008 at the University of Antwerp. Paul Cortois chaired the session, and I am grateful for his patience and insight. For their comments and encouragement I owe many thanks to Stephen Mulhall and William Desmond. Finally, I am indebted to the four anonymous reviewers; their remarks have made this a better article.

1. Ludwig Wittgenstein, *Philosophical Investigations*, trans. G. E. M. Anscombe (Oxford: Blackwell, 2001), § 335. Hereafter *PI*.
2. Arthur Schopenhauer, *The World as Will and Representation*, trans. E. F. J. Payne (New York: Dover Publications, 1966), vol. 1, 35. Hereafter cited in the text as *WWR* I (first volume), *WWR* II (second volume).
3. Arthur Schopenhauer, *Manuscript Remains*, trans. E. F. J. Payne (Oxford: Berg, 1989), 3:24.
4. The poet's workshop is Schopenhauer's conceit, and I think a telling one. "If we could see into the secret workshop of the poets, we should find that the idea is sought for the rhyme ten times more often than the rhyme for the idea" (*WWR* II, 428).
5. "Thus either the idea is stunted for the sake of the rhyme, or else the rhyme has to be satisfied with a feeble *a peu pres*" (*WWR* II, 430).
6. Friedrich Nietzsche, *The Birth of Tragedy*, trans. Ronald Speirs (Cambridge: Cambridge University Press, 1999), 30. Hereafter cited in the text as *BT*.
7. The phrase is Sartre's, from whom I adopt the distinction between *expansive* and *retractile* forms of unification. He is commenting on modern French poetry, within a general discussion of Jean Genet. On expansive form, he writes: "We are gradually made to see in a miscellaneous collection the breaking up of a prior totality whose elements, set in motion by a centrifugal force, break away from each other and fly off into space, colonizing it and there reconstituting a new unity." The retractile, however, seeks to make externality "a nothingness, a shadow, the pure, perceptible appearance of secret unities." Jean-Paul Sartre, *Saint Genet*, trans. Bernard Frechtman (New York: Pantheon Books, 1983), 464.
8. There may be traces of this in Wittgenstein's remark: "If a lion could talk, we could not understand him" (*PI*, 190.) But—to ask the same question—what if the lion could sing?
9. Seamus Heaney, "The Makings of a Music: Reflections on Wordsworth and Yeats," in *Preoccupations: Selected Prose 1968–1978* (London: Faber and Faber, 1980), 61.
10. *Timon of Athens*, Act 1, sc. 1, lines 20–25.
11. Samuel Johnson, for instance, found this passage "very obscure. He [the Poet] seems to boast the copiousness and facility of his vein, by declaring that verses drop from a poet as gums from odoriferous trees, and that his flame kindles itself without the violence necessary to elicit sparkles from the flint. What follows next? that it, 'like a current, flies/each bound it chafes.' This may mean, that it expands itself notwithstanding all obstructions; but the images in the comparison are so ill-sorted, and the effect so obscurely expressed, that I cannot but think something omitted that connected the last sentence with the former. It is well known that the players often shorten speeches to quicken the representation; and it may be suspected, that they sometimes performed their amputations with more haste than judgment." Arthur Sherbo, ed., *Johnson on Shakespeare* (New Haven, CT: Yale University Press, 1968), 707.
12. Seamus Heaney, "The Fire i' the Flint," in *Preoccupations*, 83.
13. Seamus Heaney, "The Makings of a Music," 62; hereafter page references are cited in the text.
14. Frank Kermode writes of Ben Jonson: "When he said that Shakespeare 'wanted art' he meant the laboriously excogitated craft he himself developed, something we can admire in him but do not look for in Shakespeare. . . . He himself preferred and practiced poetry that showed the 'labour of the file'." Frank Kermode, *Shakespeare's English* (London: Penguin, 2001), viii–ix. Heaney quotes T. S. Eliot, who said of Jonson, "unconscious does not respond to unconscious; no swarms of inarticulate feelings are aroused. The immediate appeal of Jonson is to the mind; his emotional tone is not in the single verse but in the design of the whole." Seamus Heaney, "The Fire i' the Flint," 85.

15. Seamus Heaney, "The Makings of a Music," 61.
16. Stanley Cavell, *Philosophy the Day After Tomorrow* (Cambridge, MA: Harvard University Press, 2005), 48. Hereafter cited in the text.
17. Stanley Cavell, *The Claim of Reason: Wittgenstein, Skepticism, Morality and Tragedy* (Oxford: Oxford University Press, 1979), 94.
18. Stanley Cavell, *Cities of Words: Letters on a Register of the Moral Life* (Cambridge, MA: Harvard University Press, 2003), 333.
19. While I am associating Wittgenstein with the interests of the economy of speech, and the assertive strain in our relations with language, this in no way means that he also shares with Schopenhauer some picture of a metaphysical voice outside language. Though questioned pretty much throughout, it seems the seductiveness of this picture is particularly explored, for instance, in paragraphs 330 to 341 of *PI*.
20. Stanley Cavell, *Emerson's Transcendental Etudes*, ed. David Justin Hodge (Stanford, CA: Stanford University Press, 2003), 19.
21. Stanley Cavell, *Disowning Knowledge: In Six Plays of Shakespeare* (Cambridge: Cambridge University Press, 1987), 3.
22. Stanley Cavell, *In Quest of the Ordinary: Lines of Skepticism and Romanticism* (Chicago, IL: University of Chicago Press, 1988), 5.
23. Cavell, *The Claim of Reason*, 241.
24. Stanley Cavell, *The Senses of Walden* (New York: The Viking Press, 1972), 79.
25. *Ibid.*, 106.
26. Cavell, *Emerson's Transcendental Etudes*, 117.
27. *Ibid.*, 17.
28. *Ibid.*, 28.
29. Cavell, *The Senses of Walden*, 28.
30. Cavell, *Emerson's Transcendental Etudes*, 203.
31. Stanley Cavell, *A Pitch of Philosophy* (Cambridge, MA: Harvard University Press, 1994), 116.
32. *Ibid.*
33. Cavell, *The Claim of Reason*, 496.

Philosophy, Poetry, Parataxis

~ Jonathan Monroe ~

ABSTRACT *At the heart of the relationship between philosophy and poetry, and of the philosophical and the literary tout court, is the relationship between poetry and prose. In the increasingly influential work of Giorgio Agamben, whose impact continues to grow across a wide range of disciplines, the relationship between philosophy and poetry, poetry and prose, receives renewed attention and significance. Situating Agamben's philosophical, poetic prose in relation to the legacy of the prose poem from Charles Baudelaire through Walter Benjamin and Rosmarie Waldrop, "Philosophy, Poetry, Parataxis" explores the implications of what Agamben calls "whatever being" or "whatever singularity" for our understanding of the potentialities inherent in the relationship between contemporary writing practices and what Agamben calls* The Coming Community. *In contributing to the development of innovative, alternative forms of textuality at once "philosophical" and "poetic," contemporary writers such as Agamben and Waldrop share an understanding of the informing role of parataxis in inflecting philosophy and poetry, poetry and prose, toward what we might call an aesthetics and politics of apposition.*

> *Wittgenstein once wrote that 'philosophy should really only be poeticized' [Philosophie dürfte man eigentlich nur dichten] . . . As for poetry, one could say . . . that poetry should really only be philosophized.*
> —Giorgio Agamben, *Idea of Prose*

> *. . . Baudelaire sometimes did not understand in understanding himself (though he did write the prose poems, which redeem all.)*
> —Philippe Lacoue-Labarthe, *Poetry as Experience*

At the heart of the relationship between philosophy and poetry—the "quintessence," as Charles Baudelaire understood, of the literary *tout court*—is the relationship between poetry and prose. While the genre-announcing, genre-defying preface to Arsène Houssaye in Baudelaire's *Le spleen de Paris* emphasizes the creation of a *"prose poétique,"* its two concluding prose poems—"Assommons les pauvres" ("Beat Up the Poor") and "Les bons chiens" ("The Faithful Dog")—are at least as concerned with the question of a *poésie philosophique* or *philosophie poétique*.[1] The latter becomes in fact, as the collection develops

~

across its fifty-one discrete yet interlocking texts, an increasingly acute, sustained emphasis through the final ironic, genre-confounding pronouncement of its closing sentence:

And every time the poet dons the painter's waistcoat he is forced to think of faithful dogs, philosophic dogs, and of Indian summers and the beauty of women past their prime. (PS 107)

An understanding of the complex interdependence and interpenetration of philosophy and poetry, poetry and prose, lies in turn at the heart of the rich affiliation that links Baudelaire to Walter Benjamin, for whom Baudelaire is arguably the single most important writer in any genre. While it would be inaccurate to say that Benjamin's reception of Baudelaire registers the importance of the verse poems of *Les fleurs du mal* almost entirely at the expense of the prose poems of *Le spleen de Paris*, it is nevertheless a curious fact of that reception that they register in Benjamin's work in such different ways. Where Benjamin offers explicit commentary on the former, as he does also on the verse poems of Bertolt Brecht,[2] the latter do not yield similar attention. In this sense, they may appear to be of less concern, incidental, inconsequential, even invisible to the philosopher-critic's priorities. Where Baudelaire's verse poems emerge in "Paris, Capital of the Nineteenth Century," "The Paris of the Second Empire in Baudelaire," and "On Some Motifs of Baudelaire" as foundational texts of modern poetry in particular and modern literature in general,[3] if commentary is the measure of influence, the prose poems may seem in Benjamin's work an after-thought at best. In the wide range of kinds of texts Benjamin produced, however, it is clear that the prose poems make their influence felt not through direct commentary as such, but rather as models for the innovative formal strategies that characterize Benjamin's richly varied oeuvre. Rather than "comment on" Baudelaire's prose poems, Benjamin absorbs their influence and inspiration in the philosophical prose-poetic forms of such texts as "One-Way Street," "Central Park," "On the Concept of History," and *The Arcades Project*,[4] to name only a few examples.

Like Baudelaire, like Benjamin, Giorgio Agamben, perhaps the most richly linked to Benjamin among contemporary philosophers, offers one of the most reflective and engaging meditations we have, both propositionally and formally, on the relationship between philosophy and literature and, more specifically, between poetry and the philosophy of language. Yet as with Benjamin, so too with Agamben, the importance of what Barbara Johnson has aptly called Baudelaire's "second revolution"[5] does not show up in the form of commentary on the prose poems themselves, but rather, here again, in their more indirect yet no less decisive influence on the shapes and forms of Agamben's own richly varied writing practices, in such innovative philosophical prose-poetic texts as *Idea of Prose*, *Language and Death: The Place of Negativity*, and *The Coming Community*.[6]

Suddenly—O miracle! O bliss of the philosopher when he sees the truth of his theory verified!— (PS 102)

As profound as Agamben's engagement is with the terms philosophy, poetry, prose, language, that engagement is consistently mediated and constrained in ways that remain deeply ironic and limiting for how we are to think of what we might call, in the rich philosophical prose-poetic language of *The Coming Community*, poetry's "whatever being" or "whatever singularity" (CC 1–2). While not at all surprising in the context of more conventional, conservative representations of the history of poetry in general and modern and contemporary poetry in particular as a history of *verse*, one recognizes a familiar slippage and sleight-of-hand in the history of critical discourse on poetry in Agamben's shift from the more careful and accurate first sentence of the two-and-a-half page prose-poetic title text, "The Idea of Prose"—"No definition of verse is perfectly satisfying unless it asserts an identity for poetry against prose through the possibility of *enjambement*"—to the less careful, less precise, more problematic claim that *enjambement* is "the distinguishing characteristic of poetic discourse."[7] While the terminological slippage involved in the semantic chain "verse = *enjambement* = poetic discourse" would be completely unsurprising in the hands of a less erudite scholar less deeply immersed in poetological questions, there is, in effect, an amusing playfulness in Agamben's wry insistence on the distinction verse-prose, as distinct from poetry-prose, within a textual performance—at once "philosophical" and "literary"—so manifestly indebted to the history of the modern prose poem since Baudelaire. In what Agamben has called a text's "*mode* of being, its *manner* of rising forth: being such as it is" (LD 98, my emphasis), and what I have called elsewhere its "antigeneric" impulses,[8] the prose poem consistently calls into question, as Agamben knows better than anyone, the conceptual division between "poetry" and "prose" which recourse to the simpler distinction between "prose" and "verse" forever elides.

> "*What! You here...! You the ambrosia eater, the drinker of quintessences!... think of some bad poet...Think of X! Think of Z!*" (PS 94)

Looked at through the lens of its Baudelairian inflections, its Benjaminian refractions, to which genre(s) of writing may Agamben's increasingly influential body of work be said to belong? What is most interesting in Agamben's approach to such a question is not his familiar and facile terminological elision of the problem the distinction poses for the relationship between philosophy and poetry, for which the prose poems of *Le spleen de Paris* stage an encounter throughout with the keenest interest. What is arguably most intriguing, and most far-reaching in his work is not, in other words, its explicit propositional claims, which at this point in the global history of modern poetry and poetics have at best a partial validity and questionable purchase as well as a potentially limiting, even regressive effect on contemporary poetic practices, but rather the ways in which Agamben's own varied *formal* practices deliberately confound any such reduction. While the propositional *whatever* of his work may continue to affirm the reductive identity "poetry = verse," what we may call the *however* of his texts gives the lie to that identification. Such a process of formal dis-identification—the breaking apart of the identity formation "poetry-verse" and its implied opposition, "verse-prose"— allows Agamben the latitude to pursue in an elliptical, prose-poetic philosophical form a questioning of the presumed opposition between philosophy and poetry that has been such a foundational antinomy in the history of Western thought.

As long as poetry remains identified with verse, as Agamben's formal practices if not his propositions makes clear, philosophy's opposition to poetry (as verse) remains in force, however subtle and complex the negotiations "between" them. As Baudelaire understood, however, shifting the arena of poetry from verse to prose levels the playing field, allowing poetry to engage philosophy not as its historical "master"—where what is called "philosophy" claims for itself the authority to dis-possess poetry, to expel it as unauthorized discourse beyond the city gates, beyond the *polis*—but as one language game among others, with its own histories, protocols, and conventions.

As Agamben's work give us to understand, whatever-is-called-poetry and whatever-is-called-philosophy are, like all discourses, subject to change, to the perhaps radical transformations of *para-deigma*, which Agamben reminds us involves, not opposition but apposition, not over-against but adjacent to, the playfully serious "setting beside" of discourses in relation to one another, poetry and philosophy included, which Agamben calls forth through his breaking apart of the German *Bei-spiel*.

> One concept that escapes the antinomy of the universal and the particular has long been familiar to us: the example . . . . Neither particular nor universal, the example is a singular object that presents itself as such, that shows its singularity. Hence . . . the Greek term, for example: *para-deigma*, that which is shown alongside (like the German *Bei-spiel*, that which plays alongside). Hence the proper place of the example is always beside itself, in the empty space in which its undefinable and unforgettable life unfolds . . . . Exemplary being is purely linguistic being . . . not defined by any property, except by being-called . . . . Hence . . . Being-called . . . is also what can bring . . . radically into question. It is the Most Common that cuts off any real community. Hence the impotent omnivalence of whatever being . . . . These pure singularities communicate only in the empty space of the example . . . . They are expropriated of all identity . . . Tricksters or fakes, assistants or 'toons,' they are the exemplars of the coming community." (CC 9–11)

Can such a passage escape registering as exemplary for the methodologies of virtually all disciplines? Is its exemplary example a concern of whatever-is-called-philosophy any more or less than of whatever-is-called-poetry, despite the antithetical, agonistic character of what is so often presumed—these days as an increasingly entrenched matter of academic bureaucracy—to be their relation, despite, "for example," the claim of another multigenre, transdisciplinary thinker, Edouard Glissant, that poetics represents "the highest point of knowledge"?[9] As Ludwig Wittgenstein, another of Agamben's major influences along with Benjamin, has given us to understand, *examples determine and define* as much as they confirm a given philosophy's or theory's claims, *as given*. Whether Edgar Allan Poe, Paul Valéry, or Gerard Manley Hopkins for Ramon Jakobson, Alexander Pushkin for Mikhail Bakhtin, or Dante and other verse poets from the Italian tradition for Agamben, the examples chosen to represent poetry come to determine and delimit whatever-is-called-poetry by definition.

In poetry, as in philosophy, what is at stake in the game is thus all in the example(s), in the *Bei-spiele*, in the *play* of examples, that "studious play" Agamben writes is "the passage that allows us to arrive at that justice that one of Benjamin's posthumous fragments defines as a state of the world in which the world appears as a good that absolutely cannot be appropriated or made juridical (Benjamin 1992, 41)," the "task of study, of play" that has as its goal "liberation."[10] It is above all this shared interest in liberating (textual) practices of "studious play"—in philosophical, prose-poetic investigations of the exceptions that prove the rules and the rules that prove the exceptions, in how much play the discursive system ("philosophy," "poetry") will allow within and between and among discourses, in how writing and community might be *otherwise*—that links Agamben's varied writing practices to those of Baudelaire and Benjamin.

> *Fascination of logical syntax. 'If—then.' 'Because.' But... undermine the certainty and authority of logic by sliding between frames of reference...*[11]

In thinking further Agamben's contributions to our understanding of relations between philosophy and literature, and by implication of the aesthetic and the political, what kinds of responses do his works open onto, how varied are the modalities they inspire? Not surprisingly, given his work's conceptual range and sophistication, responses to his rich and varied textualities tend to focus on a range of abstract concepts and propositional claims, most of which are signaled, in "philosophical" fashion, by the titles of the works themselves. While the subtitle of *Potentialities: Collected Essays in Philosophy*,[12] a work drawn from many sources in the original Italian, explicitly markets its author as a philosopher, Agamben's appeal, what might even be called at this point in his reception his "exemplarity," clearly resides in part in the range of disciplines his texts engage, from philology, linguistics, poetics, literary criticism and theory to anthropology, theology, philosophy, history, law, politics, zoology, and biology. Whatever disciplinary (dis)identifications Agamben's works suggest, their exemplarity or representativeness continues to draw a remarkable and increasing range of audiences to which few writers of such complexity can aspire. Whatever their disciplinary affiliations, scholars find in Agamben an author whose work is among the most responsive in the first decade of the twenty-first century to the most complex elucidations and elaborations of what is commonly called "critical commentary."

To respond in such a way, to emphasize the conceptual *what* or *whatever* of Agamben's texts, whatever is perceived to be their propositional singularity, is itself to respond "philosophically," to elevate the concept or Idea(s) of his texts to the place of greatest value, to attribute their importance to their place in a history of such emphases, where preeminent value is attributed less to the *how* or *however* of his texts, or what we might call their "poetics," than to their ideational content. Like the works of Baudelaire, Benjamin, and others to whom his textual strategies are most indebted, however— Nietzsche, Heidegger, Wittgenstein, Barthes, Derrida—Agamben's richly varied oeuvre is engaging in part in the extent to which it seems to invite something other than over- and predetermined, preemptive, institutionally authorized forms of response. At the heart of the *whatever* singularities of the propositional claims his works both put to work and put into play, the varied *forms* of his work perform a resistance to serviceable ideological reduction, preferring not to be instrumentalized, in the service of *whatever* discursive, disciplinary, ideological, theoretical, political agenda(s), but rather, on behalf of a "coming community" that would have much in common with the resolutely, protectively un-finished potentialities Jean-Luc Nancy calls a *communauté désoeuvrée*,[13] to be put into play. Complicating any and all acts of critical appropriation and expropriation that would turn his texts into the rule that excludes the exception, *The Coming Community* thus announces a *parti pris* on behalf of Love, we might say "against all odds" of a properly "critical" expectation, skepticism, and response. In so doing, it respects and defers, both suspends and shows deference to, the reader's freedom to prefer a more "philosophical" or "scholarly" or "poetic" or "political" or "other" response or responsiveness. Most importantly and decisively, through its own elliptical, paratactic strategies, *The Coming Community* enacts a refusal to become anyone's or any ideology's, any Idea's Example.

> *Poor Socrates had only a censor; mine is a great affirmer, mine is a Demon of action, a Demon of combat.* (PS 102)

Closely related both conceptually and formally to another philosophical, prose-poetic text indebted to Baudelaire's prose poems, Roland Barthes's *A Lover's Discourse*,[14] *The Coming Community* offers an alternative to habitual understandings and practices of critical, theoretical, philosophical commentary as confrontation and domination, that ritualistic reproduction-in-performance of a certain violence of acts of reading and writing which Jacques Derrida has called by the name "the law of genre" and Peggy Kamuf "the division of literature."[15] Along with the separation of literature and philosophy which continues to reproduce within the academy the Platonic expulsion of the poetic from the philosophical and the political, the recent history of such institutionally-enforced divisions within the humanities in the United States has led to the enormously consequential division of whatever-is-called-writing into the often now deeply entrenched, mutually incommunicable isolation of the fields that have come to be called "composition," "creative writing," and "critical theory," each with its own self-protective, identity-enforcing territorial turf.

> *I saw that antique carcass . . . beat me to a pulp.* (PS 102)

In *The Coming Community*, Agamben doesn't so much "confront" the institutionalized violence of such bureaucratically amenable Aristotelian distinctions and compartmentalizations as offer, in the name of Love—that naked, philosophically, or as we say "critically" indefensible, hopelessly naïve "concept"—a stunning, perhaps at times infuriating, yet nonetheless disarmingly innovative opening up of potentialities for the *however* as well as the *whatever* of writing. Preferring the development of such potentialities to the ritualized responses and institutionally-enforced practices of certain modes of "critical" response—the first law of which might be something like "Thou shalt not love," or "Thou shalt not give in to love," or "Thou shalt not openly embrace love," or at least "Even in embracing love, Thou shalt not be other than skeptical"—the philosophical, poetic prose of *The Coming Community* affirms from the outset the value of "whatever being," "whatever singularity," as the *sine qua non* of all that follows:

> The Whatever in question here relates to singularity . . . The singularity exposed as such is whatever you want, that is, lovable. Love is never directed toward this or that property of the loved one . . . The lover wants the loved one with all of its predicates, its being such as it is . . . . Thus, whatever singularity (the Lovable) is never the intelligence of some thing, of this or that quality or essence, but only the intelligence of an intelligence of an intelligibility. The movement Plato describes as erotic anamnesis is the movement that transports the object not toward another thing or another place, but toward its own taking-place—toward the Idea. (CC 1–2)

What is lovable in Agamben's texts, the pleasure(s) that are there for the reader to engage and prefer in them are bound up—like those of Barthes, Benjamin, Wittgenstein,

Heidegger—with the elliptical, with resistance to closure, with the placing of what is called a "thesis" *in play*. Where the thesis in its more conventional, agreed-upon argumentative manifestations ("philosophical," "critical") demands illustration, linear progression, a certain narrative of concepts—"teleological," "dialectical," "Hegelian," etc.—*The Coming Community* enacts its resistance to submission to the divisions and laws of genre, of whatever genre—whether it be called "philosophy" or "philology" or "criticism" or "poetry"—most tellingly and compellingly not in its richly nuanced unpacking of thetic claims of whatever variety, but in what we might call, both within and between and among its discrete yet interconnected amorous-philosophical-theological-political-prose-poetic texts, its *para-tactic*, or *appositional* syntax or structure. If the dream of philosophy is, as Derrida has fairly observed, denotation—the law of referential-linguistic correspondence or equivalence that imposes the linear-narrative "one word, one thought, one meaning, one thing"—the conventional goal of what is called philosophical or critical commentary is to subject the texts they comment "on" to a masterful reduction. However elliptical a strategy a text may deploy, however elliptical a role a text may invite its reader to play, commentary, understood as mastery, willingly relinquishes the reader's freedom to play in favor of a reduction of the text to a set of examples. With each "exemplary" illustration, commentary runs the risk of the reduction, or rather more typically, as Agamben understands, actively aspires to reducing, the *whatever* qualities of the text at play to non-singular conformity to the laws of genre, to its histories, protocols, and conventions.

Complicating critical reductions of the law of genre and what is called the "force" of the example, the elliptical, paratactic, appositional form of *The Coming Community*—with its radically unpredictable, anti-linear succession of discretely titled, conceptually-linked, unlinked, disjoint philosophical, prose-poetic texts; its luxurious use of "useless" space; its intricate pagination and abrupt shifts of register and focus; its invitation to the reader, both within and between and among texts, to provide the "missing links" in the "empty spaces" where everything of *para-deigmatic* importance happens, where the potentialities of redemption happen, the interruptions that open onto the transformative thought take place; its studiously playful, conceptual, philosophical, prose-poetic attention to the content of the form and the form of the content; its between and both/and neither/nor, linked-and/as-unlinked structure—furthers the poeticizing of philosophy and the philosophizing of poetry which Agamben follows Wittgenstein in developing, not merely as proposition but as (per)form(ance), as unrepeatably singular textual event, the text as "Trickster" (of philosophy) or "fake" (as poetry, literature), and vice-versa, un- or a- or other-than professional "assistant," comedic "'toon'", less static "exemplar" than *metteur-en-scène, metteur-en-jeu* ("in all seriousness") of the coming community (to become).

He swore that he had understood my theory, and that he would follow my advice. (PS 103)

Exemplifying this spirit of "studious play" both propositionally and formally in the philosophical prose poem "Certainties"—the seventh of eleven philosophical prose poems that make up the title sequence of her recent *Blindsight*—Rosmarie Waldrop inflects the liberating textual practices of Baudelaire, Benjamin, and Agamben toward what we may call "radical parataxis," or what I have called elsewhere "appositional" poetics:

> Our capacity for learning is closely concerned with memories of milking cows. Nothing repeats itself except history. The palace, in winter. Now that long sentences are in disuse, blood is not diverted into causes. Nor does the gesture of shivering produce the sensation of labor pains. The first picture of a person wearing spectacles is in a fresco of 1352.[16]

If the privileged modality of philosophy's dream of denotation is that of what Waldrop here calls "long sentences"—the informing principle of which, opposition, the dialectic, has so often tragically led to "blood" being "diverted into causes"—the dream of what is called "literature," or the literary, or a poetics, is a dream that invites us to celebrate that long sentence's "disuse," its interruption into connotation, diacritics, apposition. Placing philosophy (as hypotaxis) and poetry (as parataxis), not in opposition to each other (where no identity can be assumed in advance in either case) but rather, as Waldrop does consistently in her work, *in play* with each other, so that each ends up in a relation of being "beside itself," Waldrop's appositional procedures "prefer not to" participate in, contribute to, and consolidate the very mythology, or philosopheme, of opposition in relation to which the literary, the connotative, the diacritical, the appositional conventionally positions itself.

Preferring to be "other than" oppositional, Waldrop's philosophical prose-poetic texts set in motion an open-ended, participatory process between text and reader—akin to that of Agamben's philosophical prose-poetic "Bartleby" and other texts in *The Coming Community*—that "prefers not to" succumb to the (call it "hypotactic-Hegelian") "long sentences" of dialectical reduction.

> If philosophy is presented from the beginning as a 'confrontation' . . . and a divergence from . . . poetry (we should not forget that Plato was a tragic poet who decided to burn his tragedies at a certain point, and, seeking a new experience of language, composed those Socratic dialogues that Aristotle mentions alone with the Mimes of Sophrones as a true and proper literary genre), then what is the extreme experience of language within the poetic tradition? Do we find in the poetic tradition, unlike the philosophical tradition, a language that does not rest on the negative foundation of its own place? And where do we encounter something like a reflection on the taking place of language in the Western poetic tradition? ("The Seventh Day," LD 66)

In cultivating her characteristic procedure of what we might call paratactic-hypotaxis, or hypotactic-parataxis, the appositional approach of "breaking apart" language within, between, and among sentences, paragraphs, and texts which she has called "gap gardening" ("Why Do I Write Prose Poems," D 262), Waldrop exemplifies in her ways, as Agamben in his, what is increasingly becoming (to borrow and inflect Raymond Williams' useful formulation) the emerging dominant of our times. As the infinite linkages and linkability of the World Wide Web teach us with increasing undeniability, far from being a- or anti- or non- referential, as it has often been accused of being, such an approach is in effect nothing other than a new realism, whether in what-is-called-philosophy, or what-is-called-poetry, or whatever-in-between, or otherwise. To E. M. Forster's "Only connect!" the Web answers: "Just try not to!".

In such an inexhaustible, infinitely malleable discursive environment, as both Agamben and Waldrop help us see, the eroding, imploding, or exploding boundaries of what-is-called-philosophy and what-is-called-poetry "bleed" into each other from within as well as between and among sentences, within as well as between and among what-are-called-texts. A philosophical poetry, or poetic philosophy, of parataxis, apposition, adjacency, the disjunct, the discontinuous, slide and slippage, is, for our times, at once the highest and most grounded mimesis. As such, such work calls us to place into conversation, if not in question, the "naturalness" of what-is-called "critical" response, including such terms as "exposition" and "elucidation," the ways in which such terms over-determine what is presumed to be the character and effectivity of response (as unknowable, not given, in advance), and the ways various forms of response—call them "philosophical," call them "poetic"—produce (code "masculine") or engender (code "feminine") certain "effects" or "affects" as intentional categories.

> The originary event of poetic language . . . seems singularly close to the negative experience of the place of language that we encounter as fundamental in the Western philosophical tradition . . . . The poetic and philosophical experiences of language are thus not separated by an abyss, as an ancient tradition of thought would have it, but both rest originally in a common negative experience of the taking place of language. Perhaps, rather, only from this common negative experience is it possible to understand the meaning of that scission in the status of language that we are accustomed to call poetry and philosophy; and thus, to understand that which, while separating them, also holds them together and seems to point beyond their fracture. ("The Seventh Day," LD 74)

"Thinking," Benjamin tells us in the eighth philosophical prose-poetic section of "On the Concept of History, "involves not only the movement of thoughts, but their arrest as well."[17] Yet where the form of this disruption, or interruption, for Benjamin's masculine-history-materialist-dialectician, calls us to "blast a specific era out of the homogeneous course of history; thus, [to] blast[s] a specific life out of the era, a specific work out of the lifework" "as a result of" which "method," "the lifework is both preserved and sublated in the work, the era in the lifework, and the entire course of history in the era," Agamben's and Waldrop's preferences for (a-)dialectical, paratactic, appositional procedures suggest that what Benjamin calls the "nourishing fruit of what is historically understood," which "contains time in its interior as a precious but tasteless seed," may be running out of time. In the forms of their work, as well as in their propositional claims, both call us to understand that in our era, there is little chance such "nourishing fruit" will come to fruition unless and until we can welcome and embrace more paratactic procedures, an aesthetics, ethics, and politics of apposition, of the *Bei-spiel*, of adjacency, where the *Bei-spiele* of what-are-called philosophy and poetry exemplify writing and reading, living, learning, and loving, as "studious play" alongside:

> *cultivate the cuts, discontinuities, ruptures, cracks, fissures, holes, hitches, snags, leaps, . . . emptiness inside the semantic dimension. Inside the sentence. Explode its snakelike beauty of movement.* ("Why Do I Write Prose Poems," D 262)

As all histories are histories of inclusions and exclusions, of hierarchies, distinctions, and exceptions, supplements and subordinations, the history of philosophy, as of poetry, is a history of a discourse, like all discourses, that can't be precisely named, that is uncertain, changeable, variable, historically situated, subject to revision. That being said, in and since its Socratic articulation, philosophy has understood itself, with some degree of insistence and persistence, as itself, in what we may call with Agamben its singular *whatever* discursive being, a state of exception within the broader discursive field, the at once finite and infinite field of all discourses, as an exclusionary discourse, a discourse of distinction through which the literary, poetry, *Dichtung*, comes to find itself, *by definition*, on the outskirts of the polis, at its margins. Poetry is in that sense an impoverished discourse—not sharing the privileges of the state of/as exception—and a discourse of poverty, a minority discourse without a key that nonetheless has the power to unlock, as Roman Jakobson understood poetry, the po(v)e(r)ty, almost a *vers*, almost but not quite a verse or averse, to the state's own interests, to the interests of the exception. Poetry, in Agamben's logic, is thus aligned with others at the margins and with a "minor literature," of which the prose poem is modernism's exemplary form.

> *...gaps would have to remain gaps rather than be filled in. To point at negative space, at what eludes the grip of language. On the other hand, they could allow a sense of possibility. And, after all, discontinuity is the natural state.*
>
> ("Between, Always," D 269)

Whatever it is that goes by the name "poetry," whatever has been called poetry, in Friedrich Schlegel's words, "at any given time and place,"[18] never quite forgets, is never quite allowed to forget, that philosophy establishes and maintains its own discursive status and regimen, its own performative prestige, on its foundational exclusion of what is called poetry as the other of philosophy, as its opposite, not as an alternative discourse the polis might welcome, as for example the discourses of politics, economics, mathematics, with which the discourse of philosophy might cohabit in discursive harmony, not as a discourse, in other words, in apposition to other discourses, but a discourse in relation to which the discourse of philosophy pronounces itself opposed.

If philosophy is the necessary state of discursive exception on the basis of which the state founds its exceptional, exclusionary authority (a *Grund*, as Derrida has argued, that is also an abyss, a falling away of the ground, an *Abgrund*),[19] poetry is the discourse that compounds and confounds the named exception, the exception to the exception that strains the rule, the supplement that is posited or posed—but does not necessarily posit or pose itself—as opposite, by apposition. Expelled beyond the city gates, poetry is that discourse that refuses to accept its condition as other, that insists instead on the potentialities of being and becoming, in Edouard Glissant's indispensable formulation, of a positing, posing, performing not against or opposed to, but "in relation."

> The 'confrontation' that has always been under way between poetry and philosophy is...much more than a simple rivalry.... Philosophy, which is born precisely as an attempt to liberate poetry...finally manages to...transform it, as 'spirit,' ...but this spirit (*Geist*)...the negative (*das Negative*)... [which] belongs to...the philosophers, according to Plato, is a voice without sound. (For this reason, perhaps neither poetry nor philosophy, neither verse nor prose, will ever be able to accomplish their millennial enterprise by themselves. Perhaps only a language in which the pure prose of philosophy would...break apart...the poetic word, and in which...poetry

would...bend the prose of philosophy into a ring, would be the true human language.) ("The Seventh Day," LD 78)

If what is most characteristic, exceptional, distinctive, effective, impactful in Agamben's work is, as I've suggested less its propositional "content," the concern par excellence historically of what has called itself philosophy, than the form of its propositions, the appositional strategies Agamben deploys place philosophy in poetry's discursive proximity, opening the city gate to a conversation more among than between.

While (hypotactic) themes (concepts) drawn from Agamben's works tend not surprisingly to take precedence over their forms, especially in certain contexts—e.g. the academic dissertation, where parataxis, the deliberate, insistent interruption and disruption of thought that makes Agamben's work so interesting, is virtually by definition discouraged, even disallowed, with perhaps very real implications for that genre's viability in a sound-bitten world—the forms of his work suggest, like Waldrop's, that the eventfulness of texts of *whatever* genre is all in the gap. In the discursive economy of the contemporary university, which as everyone knows no longer remotely resembles that of a bucolic "ivory tower" pastoral ecology but an acutely stressed environment under duress, the situation of poetry and philosophy, of philosophy and literature, of the humanities generally, as between and among disciplines in the humanities and the physical and social sciences, is no freer, no less overdetermined, hierarchical, commodified, and regulated than that of the general economy. From this perspective, "poetry" and "philosophy," "philosophy" and "literature" come to understand themselves increasingly not as separate or apart, but as operating in fragile, interrelated, semi-autonomous spheres surrounded by a deepening abyss of (Un)Reason, an *Abgrund* of arbitrary power relations barely masked as "Rational."

In its bureaucratically (dys)functional separation of what is called "philosophy" from what is called "literature"—lacking differentiation from what is called "poetry in the German *Dichtung*—the academy stages an agonistic encounter that is in fact perennially, by a process of disciplinary division and/as definition/identity formation, irresolvable, not as a conceptual matter but as a built-in structural effect: philosophers are not poets, and poets are not philosophers. Those are the rules that admit no exceptions, or not many, or only a few, or maybe one.

> The 'state of emergency' in which we live is not the exception but the rule.... The current amazement that the things we are experiencing are 'still' possible...is *not* philosophical.... This amazement is not the beginning of knowledge unless it is the knowledge that the view of history which gives rise to it is untenable. (CH XIII, 392)

> The angel of history...sees one single catastrophe, which keeps piling wreckage upon wreckage and hurls it at his feet.... What we call progress is this *storm*. (CH IX, 392)

What is perhaps most representative, most exemplary, and at the same time most symptomatic about Agamben's writing, from a disciplinary and transdisciplinary perspective, is not the way it offers solutions to contemporary problems but the acuteness of the questions it asks in a global academic discursive economy where, as Benjamin reminds us in "On the Concept of History," the state of emergency, for most everyone, is not the exception but the rule, the habitual structure of radical inequity and injustice that is the foundation of what Henri Lefebvre has called the "structure of everyday life,"[20] which may appear to be hypotactic, cohesive and coherent as a Miltonic sentence, but is in reality, for the majority of the world's citizens, acutely paratactic, broken, lacking manifest coherence, the fractured syntax of which is the form of its elliptical content and the content of its motivated form, like a poem, a line, a phrase, even a (broken) word of Paul Celan, expelled, like poetry, from the city's gate, far from the privileges of prose, of the *polis*, surviving on the margins in a manner appropriate to the idea of a "minor literature" (of which the prose poem is the classic example, that "redeems all").

The struggle of syntax in Agamben's work, the way in which the syntax of his work is emblematic, representative, exemplary, symptomatic, perhaps, if we're lucky, even indexical, of our times, is the struggle between hypotaxis and parataxis, between opposition and apposition, confrontation and cohabitation, antagonism and adjacency. At its most affecting, which is also its most intellectually interesting, innovative, arresting, the elliptical character of Agamben's writing encourages not only the flow of thought but its disruption. Its empty, in-between spaces reveal and make possible a participatory opening where the coming community remains unmade, in the making, in all its potentialities, where new *para-deigmas*, new *Bei-spiele*, new readings and writings may dwell.

NOTES

1. Charles Baudelaire, "Loss of a Halo ("Perte d'auréole"), 94; "To Arsène Houssaye" ("A Arsène Houssaye"), ix–x; "Beat Up the Poor" ("Assommons les pauvres"), 101–3; and "The Faithful Dog" ("Les bons chiens"), in *Paris Spleen* (1869), trans. Louise Varèse (New York: New Directions, 1970); *Le spleen de Paris, Oeuvres completes*, ed. Claude Pichois, 2 vols. (Paris: Gallimard, Editions Pléiade, 1975); subsequent references within the text are to PS.
2. Walter Benjamin, "Commentary on Poems by Brecht," in *Selected Writings, Volume 4, 1938–1940*, trans. Edmund Jephcott and others, ed. Howard Eiland and Michael W. Jennings (Cambridge, MA: Belknap Press, 2003), 215–50.
3. Walter Benjamin, "Paris, Capital of the Nineteenth Century," "The Paris of the Second Empire in Baudelaire," and "On Some Motifs in Baudelaire," in *The Writer of Modern Life: Essays on Charles Baudelaire*, trans. Howard Eiland, Edmund Jephcott, Rodney Livingston, Harry Zohn, and Michael W. Jennings, ed. Michael W. Jennings (Cambridge, MA: Belknap Press, 2006), 30–45, 46–133, and 170–210, respectively.
4. Walter Benjamin, "One-Way Street," in *One-Way Street and Other Writings*, trans. Edmund Jephcott and Kingsley Shorter (London: Verso, 1985), 45–104; "Central Park," in *The Writer of Modern Life*, 134–69; "On the Concept of History," in *Selected Writings, Vol. 4*, 389–400; *The Arcades Project*, trans. Howard Eiland and Kevin McLaughlin (Cambridge, MA: Belknap Press, 1999).
5. Barbara Johnson, *Défigurations du langage poétique: La seconde révolution baudelairienne* (Paris: Flammarion, 1979).
6. Giorgio Agamben, *The Coming Community* (Minneapolis, MN: University of Minnesota Press, 1993), and *Language and Death: The Place of Negativity*, trans. Karen E. Pinkus with Michael Hardt (Minneapolis, MN: University of Minnesota Press, 1991) are subsequently referred to within the text as CC and LD.
7. Giorgio Agamben, *Idea of Prose*, trans. Michael Sullivan and Sam Whitsitt (Albany, NY: SUNY Press, 1995), 39.
8. Jonathan Monroe, "Introduction: The Prose Poem as a Dialogical Genre," in *A Poverty of Objects: The Prose Poem and the Politics of Genre* (Ithaca, NY: Cornell University Press, 1987),

26. See also "Baudelaire's Poor: The *Petits poèmes en prose* and the Social Reinscription of the Lyric," in *A Poverty of Objects*, 93–124, and "Syntextural Investigations," in *Poetry, Community, Movement*, ed. Jonathan Monroe, *Diacritics* 26.3–4 (Fall-Winter 1996): 126–41.

9. Edouard Glissant, *Poetics of Relation*, trans. Betsy Wing (Ann Arbor, MI: University of Michigan Press, 1997), 140.

10. Giorgio Agamben, *State of Exception*, trans. Kevin Attell (Chicago, IL: University of Chicago Press, 2005), 64.

11. Rosmarie Waldrop, "Why Do I Write Prose Poems," in *Dissonance (if you are interested)* (Tuscaloosa, AL: University of Alabama Press, 2005), 263; subsequent references within the text to *Dissonance* are to D, including those to both "Why Do I Write Prose Poems" and "Between, Always," 260–64 and 265–73, respectively.

12. Giorgio Agamben, *Potentialities: Collected Essays in Philosophy*, trans. and ed. Daniel Heller-Roazen (Stanford, CA: Stanford University Press, 1999).

13. Jean-Luc Nancy, *The Inoperative Community*, trans. and ed. Peter Connor (Minneapolis, MN: University of Minnesota Press, 1991).

14. Roland Barthes, *A Lover's Discourse: Fragments*, trans. Richard Howard (New York: Hill & Wang, 1978).

15. Jacques Derrida, "The Law of Genre," trans. Avital Ronell, *Glyph* 7 (1980): 202–29, and *Critical Inquiry* 7.1 (Autumn 1980): 55–81; Peggy Kamuf, *The Division of Literature, or, The University in Deconstruction* (Chicago, IL: University of Chicago Press, 1997).

16. Rosmarie Waldrop, "Certainties," in *Blindsight* (New York: New Directions, 2003), 88.

17. Walter Benjamin, "On the Concept of History," in *Selected Writings*, vol. 4, 396, subsequently cited within the text as CH.

18. Friedrich Schlegel, "Athenäums-Fragmente," *in Charakteristiken und Kritiken I (1796–1801)*, ed. Hans Eichner, and vol. 2 *Kritische Friedrich-Schlegel-Ausgabe*, ed. ErnstBehler (Paderborn: Ferdinand Schöningh, 1967), 182; Friedrich Schlegel's "Lucinde" and the *Fragments*, trans. Peter Firchow (Minneapolis, MN: University of Minnesota Press, 1971), 171, quoted in Monroe, "*Universalpoesie* as Fragment: Friedrich Schlegel and the Prose Poem," in *A Poverty of Objects*, 45.

19. Jacques Derrida, "The Principle of Reason: The University in the Eyes of Its Pupils," *Diacritics* 13.3 (1983): 3–20.

20. Henri Lefebvre, *Critique of Everyday Life*, 3 vols., trans. John Moore and Gregory Elliott (New York: Verso, 2008).

Emphasising the Positive: The Critical Role of Schlegel's Aesthetics

∼ JAMES CORBY ∼

ABSTRACT *In its relationship with that which might be considered to exist beyond the perceived limits of philosophical discourse—for the sake of brevity let us call it the Absolute—Early German Romanticism tends to be presented either as mystically positivistic and therefore wholly unphilosophical, or as philosophically informed and committed to a sort of critical antifoundationalism that offers, at best, a negative non-relation to the Absolute. Naturally enough, these two opposing positions give rise to opposing reconstructions of Romantic aesthetics. Whilst broadly in agreement with the latter interpretation, this article argues, in relation to Friedrich Schlegel, that in the rush to establish the philosophical credentials of* Frühromantik, *some of its complexity has been jettisoned and along with it a more accurate understanding of the guiding spirit of Romantic aesthetics. Drawing on Fichte and Walter Benjamin, it will be argued that Schlegel's notion of the* Wechselerweis *is intended to bridge the ideal and the real in a positive experience of negation and that his much-vaunted aesthetics amounts to an attempt to develop a philosophico-literary form that would be able to express or, rather, perform precisely this.*

The ongoing re-evaluation of the philosophical bearing and import of early German Romanticism has recently resolved into two divergent positions. On the one hand there is the interpretation associated with Frederick Beiser that posits the likes of Novalis and Friedrich Schlegel as idealists of a strongly Platonic bent.[1] On the other, there is the position most notably articulated by Manfred Frank, which characterises the Romantics as ontological and epistemological realists.[2] Beiser criticises Frank's interpretation of the Romantics for being caught up in what he considers to be a contradiction. Beiser suggests that, on the one hand, Frank locates the origins of early German Romanticism in the Kantian Copernican turn, the point at which correspondence theories of truth give way to constructivist theories of truth, suggesting that the subject "constitutes the very structure of reality through its activity."[3] On the other hand, though, Frank argues that Romanticism should not be interpreted as a poetic version of Kantian or Fichtean idealism. But, asks Beiser, if the Romantics reject the idea that the subject is the first principle of philosophy and instead seek a foundation in an absolute transcending it, how can it be possible to maintain that the source of Romantic aesthetics lies in Kant's

∼

constructivist conception of truth? The difficulty here, however, is Beiser's and it results from his misinterpretation of why the Copernican turn might be considered the crucial spark that ignited the Romantic flame. Beiser suggests that according to the traditional interpretation, to which he thinks Frank at least partially adheres, the Copernican turn "allowed the romantics to give metaphysical status to art." That is to say, once introduced to the idea that we construct the world we experience, the Romantics draw the conclusion that "the artist's creative activity was part of that general activity by which the subject creates its entire world."[4] Furthermore, since this process of creation cannot be fully articulated philosophically, "the romantics' first principle is suprarational and presentable only in art."[5]

Whilst this reading might well accord with traditional interpretations of early German Romanticism as irrational, it clearly amounts to a misreading when applied to Frank. For Frank, the Copernican turn was important to the development of early German Romanticism because it seemed to suggest that all knowledge is mired in an inescapable subjectivism. This was crucial for the Romantics insofar as they reacted against it, striving to gesture momentarily beyond that subjectivism through art. Far from glorying in their projective artistic ability, then, the Romantics attempt, in a certain sense, to flee from it, evincing both a "tendency towards realism,"[6] and what Elizabeth Millán Zaibert has called "epistemological humility."[7]

Whereas Beiser's reconstruction of Frank's argument presents Romanticism as marking a decisive rupture with the Kantian critical project, turning away from philosophy and reason towards art and mysticism, Frank in fact positions the Romantics as fundamentally committed to criticism, to the point of wanting to criticise even the projective ego to which the Copernican turn might seem to restrict us, in the hope of glimpsing the whole or Absolute denied by our limited, subjective perspective. So, whereas Beiser's interpretation of Frank presents Romantic aesthetics as able to unproblematically conjure the Absolute, thereby providing a positive though non-philosophical foundation for knowledge, in actual fact Frank presents Romantic aesthetics as set on a critical though largely negative course of antifoundationalism effected through a radical undecidability, generated in the artwork, that merely hints at the Absolute.

However, by placing more weight than Frank does on the influence of Fichte, and by drawing on Walter Benjamin's influential study of *Frühromantik*, a third interpretation of Romantic aesthetics and its philosophical motivation emerges, which, though largely in agreement with Frank, suggests that Frank does not place enough emphasis on the *positive* experience of negation at the basis of Romanticism. This can be seen particularly clearly in relation to Friedrich Schlegel's attempts to work just such an experience into a distinctly Romantic artwork by means of his philosophical adaptation of wit, allegory and irony into a new philosophico-literary form.

'ONE CAN NEVER BE TOO CRITICAL'

In the third *Athenaeum* Fragment Schlegel notes that "Kant introduced the concept of the negative into philosophy," but, he laments, "Wouldn't it be worthwhile trying now to introduce the concept of the positive into philosophy as well?"[8] It is not at all difficult to imagine such sentiments finding approval among a number of Schlegel's contemporaries.

Fichte, in the *Wissenschaftslehre*, had, after all, introduced the concept of an absolute self-positing I as a way of overcoming the Kantian "block" (as Adorno would later term it[9]), and the associated dualism that a number of contemporary critics thought marred Kant's contribution to philosophy. Schlegel, however, was dismissive of Fichte's attempt to complete Kant's critical philosophy, judging it not critical enough. Damning Fichte with faint praise and unforgiving irony, Schlegel makes this point in *Athenaeum* Fragment 281. He begins by saying that "Fichte's theory of knowledge is a philosophy about the subject matter of Kant's philosophy" but that his "critical method" is such that "it may very well be found that even formally he is a Kant raised to the second power, and the theory of knowledge much more critical than it seems to be." Fichte's "new version of the theory of knowledge" is even more critical in that it is "always simultaneously philosophy and philosophy of philosophy." "There may," Schlegel then rather mischievously suggests, "be valid meanings of the word critical that don't apply to every work of Fichte's" but in order to appreciate Fichte's critical method one must read him in a very distinctive way:

> In Fichte one has to look as he does—without paying attention to anything else—only at the whole and at the one thing that really matters. Only in this way can one see and understand the identity of his philosophy with Kant's. And besides, one can never be too critical. (202)

Fichte's philosophy, Schlegel somewhat elliptically implies, is in fact not at all critical because Fichte focuses on one idea, the supposed principle of the self-positing self, without taking into adequate account his own subjective grounds of observation. Fichte forgoes the requirement of any truly *critical* philosophy to be critical of its own formal procedure as well as of its subject matter.[10] It is only by ignoring this failure of Fichte's work (that is, by restricting oneself to "look as he does") that one can claim that it is cut from the same critical cloth as Kant's.

From *Wechselbestimmung* to *Wechselerweis*

Fichte, then, fails to introduce the "concept of the positive into philosophy," his lack of critical caution undermining his account of the absolute I. Indeed, to the extent that Fichte first lands on the idea of the self-positing I as a way of stemming the infinite regress that seemed to threaten the coherence of subjective experience whenever inherently limited subject/object reflection attempted to account for it, he is, Schlegel thought, unjustifiably presenting a negative as an argument for (if not quite proof of[11]) a positive and, as such, is guilty of a form of mysticism. Thus, Schlegel variously describes the *Wissenschaftslehre* as "an arbitrary positing of an unknowable and 'absolutely contingent' something as its beginning point," and as "a contempt for the critical limits of knowledge."[12]

Yet, Fichte was very well aware of the limitations of knowledge. Indeed, he explicitly positions his own philosophical endeavour as caught between "incapacity and demand"[13]: on the one hand there is the imperative to know the Absolute and, on the other, there is one's insufficiency to the task. Fichte's response to this situation is, at one point in the *Wissenschaftslehre*, to turn to what he calls "the wonderful productive power of the imagination,"[14] which, he suggests, "wavers in the middle between determination and nondetermination, between finite and infinite."[15] This interplay between the demand to comprehend the unconditioned and one's incapacity in the face of this demand provides a sense, Fichte suggests, of our interdetermining connection to the all-encompassing unity of the Absolute.[16]

It is then perhaps ironic that Schlegel reacts to the failings and limitations of philosophical discourse in a manner reminiscent of Fichte, turning to the creative power of the imagination and its ability to waver in-between two opposing poles of thought.[17] The difference lies in Fichte's adherence to the notion of the self-positing I which acts as an overarching first principle. Even when he realises that direct cognitive access to this first principle is not in fact possible, Fichte simply inverts his goal so that instead of seeking to account for the development of reflective thought from out of the absolute I, the (albeit impossible) task of philosophy becomes one of "exhausting" and "completing" the Absolute by means of ongoing synthesis. The self-positing I would then be something that one strives to achieve. It is this reliance on a first principle that Schlegel considered to be grossly uncritical. He thought that the impossibility of having the unconditioned knowledge that would be necessary to be able to affirm truthfully a first principle means that it is more accurate to speak of a *Wechselerweis* or "alternating proof"—a concept which, although surely influenced by Fichte's notion of reciprocal determination, is ultimately distinct from it. The Fichtean notion of interdetermination, or *Wechselbestimmung*, operates *within* the self-positing I, whereas, contrary to this, the very motivation of the notion of *Wechselerweis* is the realisation that, given the impossibility of getting back to *one* underlying principle (which, in the case of Fichte would be the self-positing I), no such uncritical claims can be made. Thus, Schlegel thought, since it is not possible to rise above reflective consciousness, acceding to a wholly objective perspective, we must be of the view that "philosophy . . . always begins in medias res" (171). As Frank aptly comments, "The beginning of philosophy is therefore not a positive principle grasped by knowledge, but rather the feeling of a lack of knowledge."[18] The structure of the *Wechselerweis* allows Schlegel to express this lack of positive knowledge through a "hovering" or "wavering" comparable with the wavering of Fichte's productive imagination.

Frank's interpretation of the *Wechselerweis*, however, might be considered to be at risk of underplaying some of the similarities between it and Fichte's *Wechselbestimmung*. In examining sources for the *Wechselerweis* Frank does of course refer to Fichte, but he does so rather dismissively, preferring to emphasise other possible influences on Schlegel.[19] Whereas Fichte is concerned with effecting a wavering between determination and the non–determined beyond the cognitive grasp of the subject—a wavering between the finite and the infinite—Frank's interest in establishing Schlegel first and foremost as an antifoundationalist, leads him to focus on the *Wechselerweis* as an undecidable alternating between two or more finite, determined poles.[20] Whilst such a reading is in a number of respects wholly valid, it might be considered to underappreciate the extent to which the matter was not, for Schlegel, simply one of negating particular instances of knowledge, but rather of momentarily rupturing the entirety of our cognitive grasp on the world in a way that would point to an unconditioned realm beyond. Such a bridging of the finite and the infinite would be closer to the spirit of Fichte's *Wechselbestimmung*. In contrast, Frank's reading of Schlegel's *Wechselerweis* as operating within the finite, subjective realm is wholly negative and therefore risks the criticism that it too readily and too complacently accepts the inevitability of idealism in the very way in which it reacts against it in the name of realism. It is this scaling back of Schlegel's metaphysical ambition whilst continuing to stress other aspects of his antifoundationalism that can invite the, albeit unwarranted, criticism articulated by Beiser that Frank presents the Romantics as "postmodernists *avant la lettre*,"[21] set simply on introducing a radical, system-smashing indeterminacy, without any hope of transcendence.

The wavering that Schlegel envisages has to articulate what he perceived to be an ultimate indeterminacy and lack underlying all philosophical discourse and, more broadly, be expressive of the finitude of human knowledge. As such, though, he thought it would constitute not merely a negative, resigned acknowledgement of man's limited intellectual condition, but also a positive move towards the unconditioned, undetermined beyond. Crucially, Schlegel believed that this transcendental hovering could not be properly achieved in philosophy per se, arguing that it must be effected in a distinct combination of philosophy and poetry that he would call "romantic."[22] By expressing or, rather, by enacting an indeterminate hovering, such a form of writing would be able to remain true to the critical imperative to a degree that supposedly critical philosophy inevitably fails to achieve. For Schlegel, then, there is a clear need for philosophy to embrace literary form: "Whatever can be done while poetry and philosophy are separated has been done and accomplished. So the time has come to unite the two" (251).[23]

THE TWO POLES OF ROMANTICISM

Believing philosophies of first principles to be chimerical, Schlegel imagines a philosophico-poetic literary form which would embody and put to work the absolute indeterminacy that reflective philosophy must, he thought, in the end confront. More than merely exposing philosophy's limitedness, this would in effect create a space in which the infinite might, as it were, announce itself. Unable to achieve this by means of philosophical discourse alone, "philosophy and poetry, the two most sublime powers in man . . . now intermingle in perpetual interaction in order to stimulate and develop each other."[24] In the "Epochs of Literature" section of *Dialogue on Poetry* in which Schlegel has Andrea make this point, Amalia responds by asking, "Is, then, everything poetry?" and, *prima facie*, this concern seems not at all unreasonable.[25] Does Schlegel's investment in the power of poetry not jettison all claim to objectivity? If this were the case then Schlegel would seem to be advocating nothing more than an aesthetic celebration of ignorance that, besides confirming the tag of rank subjectivism and mysticism that has so often beleaguered the philosophical reception of Romanticism, would appear out of tune with his dissatisfaction with "negative" philosophy and Fichtean "mysticism." If this is not the case, however, the question is: what could the sort of literary work he envisages do to disrupt the seemingly all-encompassing and inescapable subjectivity that he identifies in philosophy?

Anything more than a merely cursory examination of the matter serves to dispel the myth that Schlegel was advocating some sort of empty aesthetic subjectivism. In the *Athenaeum Fragments*, for instance, he writes: "Nothing is more wretched and contemptible than . . . sentimental speculation without any object" (177). There must also be something determinate about the work: in performing or putting to work indeterminacy, the work cannot simply renounce the common, prosaic construction of objective knowledge. The more strongly Fichtean reading of the *Wechselerweis* seems able to accommodate this more comfortably than Frank's reading would be able to. Whereas the latter suggests alternation between various different poles within the idealist realm, not allowing any one principle to emerge as apparently fundamental in what amounts to a profession of epistemological modesty and a quiet refusal to give up a belief in ontological realism, the former suggests something more ambitious, namely, an alternating or hovering *between* the real and the ideal, between the determinate and the indeterminate. This allows Schlegel to take a further step towards defining the philosophico–literary form he is proposing:

> There is a kind of poetry whose essence lies in the relation between the ideal and real, and which therefore, by analogy to philosophical jargon, should be called transcendental poetry. (195)

It is this inclusion in the proposed Romantic literary form of a determinate, apparently objective quality that leads Benjamin to characterise early German Romanticism, contrary to its reputation, as possessing a distinctly sober and prosaic quality.[26]

The *Wechselerweis*, then, appears to be taking shape as a hovering between the real, characterised as determinate and objective, on the one hand, and the ideal, characterised as indeterminate and subjective, on the other. There is a good deal of truth in this but caution must be exercised in identifying just what it is that Schlegel is presenting as real and objective. Schlegel's dissatisfaction with philosophy (and this is characteristic of German Romanticism more generally) is premised upon the strongly held belief, triggered by Kant's Copernican turn, that there is no way of rationally guaranteeing that what we take to be objective and real is as it appears, and that this is so because reflective thought is inextricably bound up with a subjective perspective (always *in medias res* and without cognitive access to first principles, the unconditioned or the Absolute). As such, what is ordinarily taken to be "real" is, from a Romantic point of view, more coherently understood as being "ideal." Indeed, for Schlegel, that which seems most objective and most real is more accurately considered to be that which is most convincingly illusory and misleading. It is precisely this "realism," and all such attendant positivisms, which the Romantic thinkers sought to uncover as idealism vulnerable to scepticism. Given the Romantic belief that rational, reflective objectivity is not ultimately possible, though, this uncovering or puncturing of positivistic rationalisms could not be effected by means of a discourse that would be straightforwardly recognisable as philosophy. It is as a response to this apparent philosophical impasse that Schlegel develops the idea of a hovering, alternating *Wechselerweis* embodied in an artwork. However, having identified the need for one of the poles of alternation in such a work to represent in some sense the real, and yet having dismissed as idealist and subjectivist those aspects of experience most commonly taken to be real or objective, the question now is what will provide the instance of the objective and the real necessary for the *Wechselerweis*?

To find Schlegel's solution to this we must look at what he posits as the alternative pole to the determinate and, as we now understand it, only seemingly objective element of the proposed *Wechselerweis*. This alternative is the indeterminate, poetic aspect of the work. There must be an uncertainty or indeterminacy built into the work which undermines the determinate aspect of the work, problematising its claim to objectivity and realism and thereby making possible a view of the extent of our idealism. Our idealism, Schlegel seems to believe, extends precisely to where our determinate (and, to some degree, *determinant*) cognitive grasp of the world fails, wracked against an irresolvable indeterminacy. It is this dynamic of determinacy and dissolution that constitutes the truly critical nature of the Romantic literary work; indeed, this "unworking" is the *work* of the work. It was Benjamin who most famously identified the importance of this concept of criticism to Romanticism. "Under the name of criticism," he wrote, "the Romantics at the same time confessed this inescapable insufficiency as necessary."[27] He saw that by enacting a process of radical self-critique the artwork partially frees itself from the subjective realm of the determinate. The Romantic artwork, then, might be said to perform the failure of rational reflection, thereby rupturing our subjective, conceptualising grasp on the world. Ironically, it is precisely this rupture, this dissolution in indeterminacy of the seemingly objective, that constitutes an "objective" moment in the artwork. This disruption of our idealism allows "reality" (conceived of as that which exists independently of our co-optive, conceptualising understanding) to be felt, albeit utterly indeterminately, as a lack. Thus, there is a "necessary incompleteness" to the work where the determinate exceeds itself towards an endlessly becoming, pure objectivity:

> Idealism in any form must transcend itself in one way or another, in order to return to itself and remain what it is. Therefore, there must and will arise from the matrix of idealism a new and equally infinite realism . . . .[28]

This explains why, for Schlegel, poetry, not philosophy, is the only true source of objectivity and realism. As he states in *Ideas* Fragment 96, "All philosophy is idealism, and there exists no true realism except that of poetry" (250); similarly, in the guise of Ludovico in the "Talk on Mythology" section of the *Dialogue on Poetry*, he writes that he searches for "an organ for communicating" realism and realises that "I can find it only in poetry, for in the form of philosophy and especially of systematic philosophy realism can never again appear."[29] But just as this realism must arise from idealism, the poetry which opens a space for objectivity must arise from philosophy and the wavering connection between the two sides, philosophy and idealism on the one side and poetry and realism on the other, must be *performed* by the work. In the *Athenaeum Fragments* Schlegel refers to such a work as "the subjective embryo of a developing object" and argues that it is transcendental since "transcendental is precisely whatever relates to the joining or separating of the ideal and the real" (164).

It should now be clear why Frank's construal of the *Wechselerweis* would be insufficient to account for such a radical aesthetic position, since its focus is too narrowly on Schlegel's more modest antifoundationalist stance, at the expense of the more fundamental *Wechselerweis* between the determined and the indeterminate. For Schlegel, the critical moment of dissolution in the artwork is not merely negative: any destruction is always accompanied by a certain creative becoming.[30] There is, of course, a negative quality inherent in Schlegel's method but this is the result of a positive reaction against subjectivism. The work is constructed to rupture subjectivity *for the sake of* a negative feeling of emerging, indeterminate objectivity, in the belief that that is the most efficacious course of action given that there can be no knowledge of the Absolute. As Schlegel says, "a negative feeling . . . is much better . . . than an absence of feeling" because "even a decided incapacity of which one is completely aware, or else a strong antipathy . . . presupposes at least a partial capacity and sympathy" (151). In this regard, it might be said that the negation is positively motivated. Schlegel makes this point, indicating the necessity of the interplay between positive motivation and a negative sense, with remarkable subtlety with *Critical* Fragment 47: "Whoever desires the infinite doesn't know what he desires. But one can't turn this sentence around" (149). This "not knowing," therefore, is not an unmotivated or innocent "not knowing." It is the *work* of the work, the positive moment of the work's self-negation.

Taking his cue from the famous *Athenaeum* Fragment 116, in which Schlegel describes how "Romantic poetry" can "hover at the midpoint between the portrayed and the portrayer, free of all real and ideal self-interest, on the wings of poetic reflection, and can raise that reflection again and again to a higher power, can multiply it in an endless succession of mirrors" (175), Benjamin suggests that this Romantic concept of criticism is, in fact, predominantly positive. He takes up the idea of "the unfolding of the spirit,"[31] "the intensification of the consciousness of the work through criticism," and suggests that "the positive moment of this heightening of consciousness far outweighs the negative":

> The moment of self-annihilation, the possible negation in reflection, cannot therefore be of much consequence over against the thoroughly positive moment of the heightening of consciousness in the one who is reflecting.[32]

The critical moment reveals the infinitude of reflection, thereby dissolving the "individual work of art . . . in the medium of art."[33] Rodolphe Gasché summarises Benjamin's interpretation thus:

> In short, then, critique in the medium of art is an objective movement in which self-limited reflection, or form, is unbounded through a potentiation of the reflection frozen in the singular work, and through which that work becomes dissolved into the medium of reflection, the continuum of forms, the idea of art itself.[34]

The individual work, therefore, moves towards universality. In *Athenaeum* Fragment 116 Schlegel says, "Romantic poetry is a progressive, universal poetry" (175), and in *Athenaeum* Fragment 451 he suggests "universality can attain harmony only through the conjunction of poetry and philosophy" (240). Holding poetry and philosophy together in abyssal reflection, the Schlegelian work *works*, hovering aporetically between idealism and realism, between the specificity of the individual work and the indeterminacy of the universal, dissolving in a process of endless becoming. This, for Schlegel, is the work, and as Lothario says in the "Talk on Mythology," "Only by being individual and universal does a work become *the work*."[35] It is in occupying both these poles of the *Wechselerweis* that the work is transcendental:

> A work is cultivated when it is everywhere sharply delimited, but within those limits limitless and inexhaustible; when it is completely faithful to itself, entirely homogeneous, and nonetheless exalted above itself. (204)

"The romantic kind of poetry," Schlegel famously says, "is still in the state of becoming; that, in fact, is its real essence: that it should forever be becoming and never be perfected" (175). But how should one characterise such a work which, on the one hand, is individual, limited, even prosaic, and yet, on the other hand, is universal, indeterminate and in a state of constant becoming where "nothing stands still, everything...developing and changing and moving harmoniously" (237)? What sort of work could be both complete and incomplete in this way? Indeed, what sort of work could actually *be* complete incompletion in the way Schlegel demands? Schlegel's focus here turns to the fragment as the form of writing most suited to meeting these requirements.[36]

WIT, ALLEGORY, IRONY, AND THE ROMANTIC FRAGMENT

In describing the fragmentary work he envisages, Schlegel identifies three aesthetic qualities as being of particular importance: wit, allegory, and irony. Rather than referring to existing understandings of wit, allegory, and irony which treat them as aesthetic qualities, Schlegel seems to want to craft completely new understandings of them as aesthetic qualities by positioning them as *philosophical* notions which must be poeticised in order to be properly operative.

In the case of wit this process is particularly clear. In *Athenaeum* Fragment 220 Schlegel identifies an "absolute, enthusiastic, thoroughly material wit" which is "the principle and the organ of universal philosophy" and which he contrasts with "the unsatisfied and evanescent expectation of purely poetical wit." He finds instances of material wit in Bacon and Leibniz, whose "whole philosophy consists of a few fragments and projects that are witty in this sense" (191–92). That he also identifies "natural syncretistic spirit and critical wit" in Kant's work is unsurprising since, as Lacoue-Labarthe and Nancy put it, "*Witz* very precisely represents an *a priori* synthesis in the Kantian sense, but one that is removed from Kant's limiting conditions and critical procedures and that involves the synthesis not only of an object but of a subject as well."[37] Schlegel goes on to say of material wit,

> The most important scientific discoveries are bon mots of this sort—are so because of the surprising contingency of their origin, the unifying force of their thought, and the baroqueness of their casual expression. (192)

Clearly, and quite provocatively, Schlegel is adding a new philosophical depth to the meaning of wit (and also, here, to the usually rather flippant and superficial phrase "*bon mot*"). So what does this transformed understanding of wit imply? Our cue here perhaps should be Schlegel's suggestion that the best instances of material wit are "*échappées de vue* into the infinite" (192). Wit is an "explosion" (153), a "lightening bolt" (243) which, in an instant, welds together two ideas the prior apparent incommensurability of which makes their union—and the subsequent clearly indubitable appropriateness of that union—all the more surprising. Showing, in a flash, connection where connection was least expected, wit's sheer synthesising force opens the possibility of unlimited connectivity, seemingly presaging absolute synthesis. And yet, because of the chaotic circumstances of individual instances of wit's synthetic ability, the suddenness in which the known order is overturned, wit is also "fragmentary genius" (144): "It has to be properly systematic, and then again it doesn't; with all its completeness, something should still seem to be missing, as if torn away" (224). Thus, in an equally weighted, and seemingly paradoxical (perhaps one should rather say *witty*) affirmation of both systematicity and chaos, wit affords us a glimpse into the infinite. This insight into the infinite, such as it is, comes to us only through our finitude and, in particular, through the momentary disruption of that finitude. The sense of the infinite we gain, then, is completely non-substantive. It is merely the unlimited potentiality made momentarily available by the sudden—disruptive but synthesising—rearrangement that takes place in our subjective grasp of the world. That there is no question of transcending our finitude, of simply leaving it behind, is something that Frank rightly makes clear: wit is the "selective flashing . . . of the infinite in the finite."[38]

With this greatly expanded, distinctly philosophical conception of wit, Schlegel clearly distances himself from the traditional idea of wit as a clever conceit the natural domain of which is urbane conversation and mannered, often superficial, literature. As has been suggested, however, Schlegel believes that philosophy has run its course in terms of what it can achieve on its own, and the task now is to join it with poetry in a new fragmentary form. Wit, as Schlegel conceives it, can be accounted for philosophically, but it is the fragment which is best suited to the actual performance of wit. Thus, one must "poeticise wit" in the form of Romantic poetry so that "Romantic poetry is in the arts what wit is in philosophy" (175).

The counterpart to this type of wit is allegory, an artistic concept which Schlegel, again, transforms by means of a philosophical interpretation. Allegory, for Schlegel, is a response to the failure of reflective inquiry to access the Absolute. The "unutterable," Schlegel has Ludovico say in "Talk on Mythology," "can be expressed only allegorically."[39] Allegory is "the mediating term between unity and multiplicity" which "results from the impossibility of reaching the Highest by reflection."[40] Allegory points beyond itself but, for Schlegel, this is not so much symbolic representation as it is the failure of symbolic representation.[41] Whereas traditional allegory partially effaces its literal sense, in order to teach a more profound lesson, Schlegelian allegory partially effaces its literal sense in order to try to open a space for an unknown and wholly indeterminate other to speak.[42]

One way of understanding Schlegel's concept of irony is to see it as combining the synthesising power of wit with the formal dissolution of the finite at work in his concept of allegory.[43] Like his understanding of wit and allegory, Schlegel's understanding of irony differs significantly from traditional interpretations of the term. In developing a form of irony which at the same time fulfils both the creative function of wit and the destructive function of allegory, he is forced to look beyond the rhetorical notion of irony, influenced by Quintillian and Cicero, and prevalent in Europe at that time. Rhetorical irony is, as one commentator puts it, "a figure of speech that means exactly the opposite of what it says."[44] Such irony can, in this way, be said to be both creative and destructive: by negating, or "destroying" one meaning or interpretation, it asserts, or "creates" another. Schlegel, though, required a form of irony in which the sense of negation and destruction is more equivocal, less predictable and less easily resolvable and which, as a result, is more profound and powerfully productive.

To develop such a form, Schlegel must first re-inscribe irony—"contrary to the entire rhetorical tradition of Europe," suggests Behler—as a philosophical notion.[45] Hence, Schlegel asserts that "philosophy is the real homeland of irony" and he speaks favourably of the "logical beauty" of the irony of the Socratic dialogue (148). This Socratic irony, wherein ignorance is feigned in order to deconstruct the interlocutor's argument thereby indirectly leading the interlocutor to a form of enlightenment, is particularly important for Schlegel. It provides him with a model of irony in which everything is "guilelessly open and deeply hidden," and in which a certain productive tension obtains:

> It contains and arouses a feeling of indissoluble antagonism between the absolute and the relative, between the impossibility and the necessity of complete communication. (156)

Having aligned himself with this philosophical understanding of irony, Schlegel begins to recast it in the form of the Romantic fragment. He thinks that a dialogue, of the type in which Socratic irony operates, "is a chain or garland of fragments" but believes that at present "no genre exists that is fragmentary both in form and content" (170). This, Hammermeister suggests, is for Schlegel something "which philosophy can understand but only art can do," and so, "to fulfil the promises of romantic philosophy," poetry itself must become ironic.[46] The real homeland of irony may be philosophy but, as with wit and allegory, irony must be poeticised. Recalling the "sublime urbanity" of Socratic irony which can release philosophy from "rigid systems," Schlegel writes: "Only poetry can also reach the heights of philosophy in this way" (148).

So, what would poeticised Socratic irony look like? Or, rather, knowing what we do about how Schlegel envisages fragmentary writing and the work of the fragment, how would poeticised Socratic irony meet the requirements of the Schlegelian fragment form? There is a strong structural similarity between the two insofar as both rely on an alternation between two poles. In a typical Socratic dialogue this is between the figure of Socrates himself, who introduces an element of uncertainty and dissimulation, and his interlocutor, who conveys the depthless clarity of received wisdom. The interplay of the two gradually leads to the latter position being undermined. The position represented by Socrates can therefore be said to be the objective stance, though this objectivity is not expressed directly or propositionally. As has been suggested, the wavering in the Schlegelian fragment is prima facie between a prosaic, determinate, objective reality and an ideal, subjective indeterminacy. The infinite reciprocation between the two poles reverses this view so that the prosaic, determinate element of the fragment is revealed as subjective and ideal and the indeterminate element becomes the source of realism and objectivity. This, it was shown, is the *work* of the Schlegelian work. It might be said, then, that in poeticising Socratic irony, besides compressing its temporality from that of a dialogue to the endlessly recurring instantaneity of a fragment, Schlegel radicalises the uncertainty, the lack of fixedness of the "Socratic" part of the dialogue, transforming it into the necessary critical indeterminacy of the fragment. Whereas the Socratic dialogue ultimately reaches what one may call a position which can claim to be both objective and determinate, Schlegelian irony "lacks," as Hammermeister puts it, this "serious conviction of the attainability of a truth that can be grasped as a concept and communicated to others."[47]

This interpretation is echoed by Charles Larmore who describes Schlegelian irony thus:

> It involves using some particular set of words to suggest the Absolute; what is not directly, but only indirectly communicated is therefore not some fully determinate thought, but rather something essentially indeterminate.[48]

For Schlegel, irony sets to work the indeterminate and the determinate in a way that is at once creative and destructive: destructive insofar as the illusion of determinacy is disclosed and creative insofar as in its place an indeterminate, objective space, a place of possibility, is opened up. To bring something to the point of irony is to bring it "to the point of continuously fluctuating between self-creation and self-destruction" (167).[49] This sort of ironic hovering between two poles is achieved through a certain naiveté of the work in which intention and instinct are held in balance. On its own, intention would fail to give any sense of the Absolute because it cannot escape the subjectivism to which its reflective conceptualising restricts it; and left entirely to instinct there would be no *work* as such:

> If it's simply instinctive, then it's childlike, childish, or silly; if it's merely intentional, then it gives rise to affectation. The beautiful, poetical, ideal naive must combine intention and instinct. (167)

Brought together, the result is a productive tension between the determinacy to which intention gives rise and the indeterminacy begotten by instinct. This, again, is inspired by Socratic irony, which, Schlegel suggests, "is the only involuntary and yet completely deliberate dissimulation" (155). Thus, despite evident differences, there is a strong familial tie between Socratic and Schlegelian irony.[50] Indeed, Schlegel's statement that Socratic irony develops from "the conjunction of a perfectly instinctive and a perfectly conscious philosophy" could just as well serve as a description of the idea that motivates his own form of irony.

This understanding of Romantic irony was endorsed by Benjamin for whom the critical moment of objectivity in the Romantic art work, which we now understand to be the radicalisation of Socratic irony, was particularly important. He acknowledges the destructive force of irony but distinguishes between "irony of the material," which he calls "negative and subjective," and "irony of the form," which he calls "positive and objective."[51] He argues that material irony is merely "irony as a sentiment of the artist"[52] and suggests that the mistaken belief that this is the irony of early German Romanticism "has encouraged the notion of a Romantic subjectivism *sans phrase*." The "ironisation of the artistic form," however, "presents an objective moment in the work itself,"[53] and it is "the peculiar positivity of this irony," Benjamin argues, which is favoured by the Romantics since "the Romantics themselves could not have experienced irony as something artistic if they had seen in it the absolute dissolution of the work":

> Not only does it not destroy the work on which it fastens, but it draws the work nearer to indestructibility. Through the destruction, in irony, of the particular form of presentation of the work, the relative unity of the individual work is thrust back deeper into the unity of art as universal work; it is fully referred to the latter, without being lost in it. . . . The ironisation of the presentation form is, as it were, the storm blast that raises the curtain on the transcendental order of art, disclosing this order and in it the immediate existence of the work as a mystery.[54]

Thus, Benjamin concludes, "formal irony is not . . . an intentional demeanor of the author . . . but must be appreciated as an objective moment in the work itself." This, he suggests, is the ironic work's "paradoxical venture: through demolition to continue building on the formation, to demonstrate in the work itself its relationship to the idea."[55]

This reading of Schlegelian irony emerges naturally from the more Fichtean reconstruction of Schlegel's *Wechselerweis*, and differs quite significantly from Frank's interpretation of Schlegel's model of irony as an interminable negation of successive finite positions.[56] The risk of Frank's interpretation is that in eliding the aspects of Romantic aesthetics least palatable to contemporary philosophical tastes, Schlegel emerges, at best, as an ironist in the mould of Rorty. This similarity between Schlegel and Rorty has been approvingly developed by Elizabeth Millán Zaibert who draws comparisons between Schlegel's antifoundationalism and Rorty's opposition to logical positivism. These comparisons are accurate and revealing as far as they go, but they are also potentially misleading. Schlegel was indeed concerned with unseating the pretensions of philosophy and in particular the philosophical quest for a founding principle, but that does not do justice to his further belief that in the resulting indeterminacy it may be possible to have some sort of experience of the Absolute, albeit one in which the Absolute remains beyond one's cognitive grasp. However, this view of Schlegel as an antifoundational ironist is wholly in keeping with Frank's view of the *Wechselerweis* which, using the metaphor Millán Zaibert adopts, comes to appear as an unending crossword puzzle.[57] In underplaying the positive experience of negation at the heart of the Romantic artwork's activation of the *Wechselerweis*, Frank's interpretation remains too negative, too cautiously pragmatic, and ironically it is perhaps this that leads Beiser to see Frank as a postmodernist interpreter of Schlegel as someone bent on cultivating a destabilising play of indeterminacy without any higher, more positive goal and at odds with Kant's critical project. Beiser's judgement here is surely erroneous, but given Frank's interpretation of the *Wechselerweis*, it is perhaps not surprising.

Beiser is right that Schlegel remains deeply influenced by idealism and Frank is right that, despite this, Schlegel, in his refusal to see the world as transparent to reason, should be considered a realist. What Beiser fails to see and what Frank does not sufficiently acknowledge is that Romanticism's negative gesturing towards a reality that remains opaque to the subjective perspective of mind becomes, by way of the critical function of the Romantic artwork, a positive and objective experience of the unconditioned, an encounter, in other words, with the real that asserts itself against the subjectivism of idealism. Much depends, then, on whether Schlegel's Romantic aesthetics can be transformed into actual artworks that deliver this experience.

'A RADIANTLY IMPROBABLE DREAM'?[58]

Schlegel's ambition to transform philosophy by joining it with literature in a new fragmentary form ended disappointingly without issue, the fragments he envisaged remaining unwritten. Schlegel imagined a fragmentary form that would suspend our finite and only seemingly objective grasp on the world and in that suspension momentarily reveal a pure, indeterminate objectivity that remains unconditioned. Such a fragment would incorporate what Lacoue-Labarthe and Nancy call "an essential incompletion"[59] and yet, as *Athenaeum* Fragment 206 puts it, "a fragment . . . has to be entirely isolated from the surrounding world and be complete in itself like a hedgehog" (189, translation modified). The criticism has been made of Schlegel's published fragments that they emphasise this subjective, hedgehog–like self–containment at the expense of objective, indeterminate incompletion. Maurice Blanchot writes:

> In truth, and particularly in the case of Friedrich Schlegel, the fragment often seems a means for complacently abandoning oneself to the self rather than an attempt to elaborate a more rigorous mode of writing. Then to write fragmentarily is simply to welcome one's own disorder, to close up upon one's own self in a contented isolation, and thus to refuse the opening that the fragmentary exigency represents; an exigency that does not exclude totality, but goes beyond it.[60]

In forsaking its essential incompletion, the fragment risks collapsing into the epigram or aphorism, "that is to say, [into] the closure of a perfect sentence."[61] Ironically, this is supported by a comment that Schlegel makes in *Athenaeum* Fragment 77, which seems to justify Blanchot's charge of complacent subjectivism:

> As yet no genre exists that is fragmentary both in form and content, simultaneously completely subjective and individual, and completely objective and like a necessary part in a system of all the sciences. (170)

It seems, then, that the complete incompletion of the fragment is yet to be achieved.

However, a further and perhaps far more intractable difficulty stands in the way of Schlegel's planned joining of philosophy and literature. Even if Schlegel had succeeded in producing such philosophico–poetic fragments that might be said to perform the *Wechselerweis*, how would he escape the accusation that far from disclosing the finitude of reflective knowledge and opening a space of pure objectivity beyond subjective control, what is in fact being demonstrated is the all–powerful mastery of the artist who produces such fragments? This criticism, articulated most famously by Hegel, roots Romanticism in a conception of subjectivity which is essentially Fichtean.[62] For Fichte, objectivity is at some level absolutely contingent upon subjectivity. It belongs to the realm of the not–I; that, in other words, which negates subjectivity. But since the "deed–act" or *Tathandlung* of the absolute ego is a positing of both self and not–self, the objective not–self must necessarily be understood as being born out of subjectivity of some sort. Such a reading of Schlegelian Romanticism threatens to entrap it within the very subjectivism from which it is trying to escape. Ultimately, without either self–validating fragmentary works or a fuller account of artistic autonomy, this, perhaps, remains the real irony of early German Romanticism.

Romanticism, then, must be—and has often been—judged to fail, and it is perhaps not unreasonable to conclude that sympathetic contemporary commentators such as Frank, keen on rendering Romanticism philosophically respectable, are inclined to focus attention away from this failure and the metaphysical ambitions that occasioned it, towards more pragmatic interpretations. The resulting picture of Schlegel's thought is perhaps less incorrect than it is out of focus and, on the whole, it is certainly more accurate than that proposed by Beiser, but ultimately the scale and complexity of Schlegel's aesthetics may be diminished by it.

NOTES

1. See, in particular, Frederick Beiser, *German Idealism: The Struggle Against Subjectivism, 1781–1801* (Cambridge, MA: Harvard University Press, 2002), and *The Romantic Imperative: The Concept of Early German Romanticism* (Cambridge, MA: Harvard University Press, 2003).
2. "If *ontological* realism can be expressed by the thesis that reality exists independently of our consciousness (even if we suppose thought to play a role in structuring reality) and if *epistemological* realism consists in the thesis that we do not possess adequate knowledge of reality, then early German Romanticism can be called a version of ontological and epistemological realism." Manfred Frank, *The Philosophical Foundations of Early German Romanticism*, trans. Elizabeth Millán Zaibert (New York: State University of New York Press, 2004), 28.
3. Beiser, *The Romantic Imperative*, 74.
4. *Ibid.*
5. *Ibid.*, 59.
6. Frank, *The Philosophical Foundations of Early German Romanticism*, 68.
7. Elizabeth Millán Zaibert, *Friedrich Schlegel and the Emergence of Romantic Philosophy* (Albany, NY: State University of New York Press, 2007), 39. Beiser clearly ignores the fact that Kant himself remained torn between a constructivist theory of truth and correspondence or representationalist theories of truth. Kant's constructivism, as well as his lingering, conflicting commitment to representationalism, is illuminatingly discussed by Tom Rockmore in *Kant and Idealism* (New Haven, CT: Yale University Press, 2007). From this perspective, it might be argued that Frank's interpretation of Romanticism grows out of the implicit belief that the Romantics simply play out this tension, convinced of being trapped within their own projections and yet unable to give up the desire for transparent access to whatever it is that those projections obscure.
8. Friedrich Schlegel, *Friedrich Schlegel's* Lucinde *and the* Fragments, trans. Peter Firchow (Minneapolis, MN: University of Minnesota Press, 1971), 161. Subsequent references to this work are cited in the text.
9. See, in particular, Theodor W. Adorno, *Negative Dialectics*, trans. E. B. Ashton (London: Routledge, 2000), 384–90.
10. Schlegel writes: "In the *Wissenschaftslehre*, the method must also be critical; but that is what Fichte is not." Quoted in Frank, *The Philosophical Foundations of Early German Romanticism*, 180.
11. "Our task is to *discover* the primordial, absolutely unconditioned first principle of all human knowledge. This can be neither *proved* nor *defined*, if it is to be an absolutely primary principle." J. G. Fichte, *Johann Gottlieb Fichte's sämmtliche Werke*, ed. I. H. Fichte (Berlin: Veit and Co., 1845–1846), 1.91.
12. Quoted in Frank, *The Philosophical Foundations of Early German Romanticism*, 180.
13. Fichte, *sämmtliche Werke*, 1.225.
14. *Ibid.*, 1.208.
15. *Ibid.*, 1.216–17.
16. For Fichte's most clear statements in this regard, see *sämmtliche Werke*, 1.215–17.
17. We know from a letter that Hölderlin wrote to Hegel that Fichte's notion of reciprocal determination (*Wechselbestimmung*) caused quite a stir (see Friedrich Hölderlin, "Letter to Hegel, 26 January 1795," trans. Stefan Bird-Pollan, in *Classic and Romantic German Aesthetics*, ed. J. M. Bernstein [Cambridge: Cambridge University Press, 2003], 190). It is likely that Schlegel was similarly influenced.
18. Frank, *The Philosophical Foundations of Early German Romanticism*, 189.
19. Frank writes: "One could think of another, much closer source of Schlegel's talk of *Wechselerweis*: Fichte's use of *Wechselbestimmung* (alternating or reciprocal determination) at the

beginning of the theoretical part of his *Wissenschaftslehre* . . . but it is clear, that the recollection of the definite use of the concept in Novalis or Fichte's thought, does not fully explain Schlegel's fundamental use of the term '*Wechselerweis*'" (*Ibid.*, 193).

20. Frank writes: "That the highest principle of philosophy can only be a *Wechselerweis* should simply mean here, that a concept or a proposition can never alone per se, that is to say from Cartesian evidence, be established; rather, it is established first through a further and second (provisional) concept or proposition (for which the same holds, so that through a coherence formation of truth we come ever closer to the truth without ever grasping it in one single thought)" (*Ibid.*, 203).

21. Beiser, *The Romantic Imperative*, 2. See also 4 and 192, note 8.

22. Schlegel's most illuminating statements about "romantic poetry" can be found in *Athenaeum* Fragment 116 (175–76). For a discussion of the words "romantic" and "romanticism," see Ernst Behler, *German Romantic Literary Theory* (Cambridge: Cambridge University Press, 1993), 24–33.

23. Schlegel reiterates this imperative numerous times. For instance, in Fragment 115 of *Critical Fragments* he writes: "poetry and philosophy should be made one," and in Fragment 48 of *Ideas*, he writes: "Where philosophy ends, poetry must begin" (translation modified) (157, 245).

24. Friedrich Schlegel, *Dialogue on Poetry*, in *Dialogue on Poetry and Literary Aphorisms*, trans. Ernst Behler and Roman Struc (University Park, PA: Pennsylvania State University Press, 1968), 74.

25. *Ibid.*, 75. For the supposed real-life identities of all the characters of the *Dialogue on Poetry*, see Philippe Lacoue-Labarthe and Jean-Luc Nancy, *The Literary Absolute*, trans. Philip Barnard and Cheryl Lester (New York: State University of New York Press, 1988), 89.

26. Walter Benjamin, "The Concept of Criticism in German Romanticism," trans. David Lachterman, Howard Eiland, and Ian Balfour, in *Selected Writings: Volume 1, 1913–1926*, ed. Marcus Bullock and Michael W. Jennings (Cambridge, MA: The Belknap Press of Harvard University Press, 1996), 175–77.

27. *Ibid.*, 143.

28. Schlegel, *Dialogue on Poetry*, 83.

29. *Ibid.*, 84.

30. Andrew Bowie emphasises the importance of the relationship between creation and destruction for philosophy of this period and, following Frank, partly attributes it to a contemporary interest in the figure of Dionysus. See Andrew Bowie, *Aesthetics and Subjectivity* (Manchester: Manchester University Press, 2003), 66–67.

31. Benjamin, "The Concept of Criticism in German Romanticism," 151.

32. *Ibid.*, 152.

33. *Ibid.*, 153.

34. Rodolphe Gasché, "The Sober Absolute: On Benjamin and the Early Romantics," in *Walter Benjamin and Romanticism*, ed. Beatrice Hanssen and Andrew Benjamin (London: Continuum, 2002), 60.

35. Schlegel, *Dialogue on Poetry*, 92.

36. For a discussion of the centrality of the fragment to Jena Romanticism, see Lacoue-Labarthe and Nancy, *The Literary Absolute*, and Simon Critchley, *Very Little . . . Almost Nothing: Death, Philosophy, Literature* (London: Routledge, 2004), 125–31.

37. Lacoue-Labarthe and Nancy, *The Literary Absolute*, 53. One could read *Ideas* Fragment 26 as supporting this view: "Wit is the appearance, the outward lightning bolt of the imagination" (243). Similarly, in "Letter About the Novel" in *Dialogue on Poetry*, the suggestion is made that "of that which originally was imagination there remains in the world of appearances only what we call wit" (100). This view is also endorsed by Frank who refers to this aspect of Schlegelian wit as "clearly a Kantian reminiscence" (*The Philosophical Foundations of Early German Romanticism*, 209).

38. Frank, *The Philosophical Foundations of Early German Romanticism*, 209.

39. Schlegel, *Dialogue on Poetry*, 90.

40. Schlegel, quoted by Andrew Bowie in *From Romanticism to Critical Theory: The Philosophy of German Literary Theory* (London and New York: Routledge, 1997), 68.

41. For an insightful discussion of allegory and symbol in relation to early German Romanticism, see Paul de Man, "The Rhetoric of Temporality," in *Blindness and Insight* (London: Routledge, 1989).

42. The word "allegory" derives from the Greek *allēgoriā*: *allos* (other) and *agoreuein* (to speak).

43. Frank, for instance, suggests that "irony is the searched for structure of the whole whose abstract parts are wit and allegory.... . Irony is the synthesis of wit and allegory" (*The Philosophical Foundation of Early German Romanticism*, 216).

44. Kai Hammermeister, *The German Aesthetic Tradition* (Cambridge: Cambridge University Press, 2002), 82.

45. Behler, *German Romantic Literary Theory*, 146. Behler goes on to remark: "Friedrich Schlegel was, of course, aware of the rhetorical tradition in which irony was transmitted and had found its habitual place in Europe. But this rhetorical irony, bound to individual instances, to particular figures, appeared to him minor and insignificant compared to the philosophical homeland of irony where it could manifest itself 'throughout'" (147).

46. Hammermeister, *The German Aesthetic Tradition*, 82. Hammermeister is emphatic: "Philosophy can describe irony, but it is art that must practise it" (84).

47. *Ibid.*, 83. Bowie makes a similar point contrasting Romantic irony with rhetorical irony: "The Romantics' wariness of determinate propositions is also what leads them to their particular conception of irony. Normally irony is the determinate negation of what is asserted in a proposition: 'That was good', said ironically, means it wasn't. Romantic irony, on the other hand, requires the negation of the assertion, but not in favour of a determinate contrary assertion" (*From Romanticism to Critical Theory*, 69).

48. Charles Larmore, "Hölderlin and Novalis," in *The Cambridge Companion to German Idealism*, ed. Karl Ameriks (Cambridge: Cambridge University Press, 2000), 156.

49. Similarly, in *Athenaeum* Fragment 121, Schlegel writes: "An idea is a concept perfected to the point of irony, an absolute synthesis of absolute antitheses, the continual self-creating interchange of two conflicting thoughts" (176).

50. With regard to Romantic irony's connection to other forms of irony, Schlegel's essay "On Incomprehensibility" is of particular importance. Here Schlegel masterfully combines rhetorical irony, quasi-Socratic irony and an attempt at Romantic irony in a dizzying piece of work which both constatively and performatively explores irony (in *Classic and Romantic German Aesthetics*, 297–307).

51. Benjamin, "The Concept of Criticism in German Romanticism," 164.

52. *Ibid.*, 165.

53. *Ibid.*, 163.

54. *Ibid.*, 164–65. There are undeniable parallels here with Beiser's rather less nuanced account of Romanticism's debt to Platonism, the exact nature of which are beyond the scope of this essay. See Beiser, *The Romantic Imperative*, 59–70.

55. *Ibid.*, 165. At approximately the same time as Benjamin, Georg Lukács was also explicitly making a connection between irony and objectivity. He suggests that "irony is the objectivity of the novel" and, famously, writes: "Irony, the self-surmounting of a subjectivity that has gone as far as it was possible to go, is the highest freedom that can be achieved in a world without God." Georg Lukács, *The Theory of the Novel*, trans. Anna Bostock (London: Merlin Press, 1971), 90, 93.

56. "In order to become comprehensible, that which is pure must limit itself; any border contradicts the essential infinity of that which is pure, however; therefore it must always overstep the limits which it sets to itself, and then limit itself again, and then overstep these limits, and so on and on" (Frank, *The Philosophical Foundations of Early German Romanticism*, 215–16).

57. Millán Zaibert, *Friedrich Schlegel and the Emergence of Romantic Philosophy*, 19.

58. Lukács said of Jena Romanticism: "It was a dance on a glowing volcano, it was a radiantly improbable dream." Georg Lukács, "On the Romantic Philosophy of Life," in *Soul and Form* (London: Merlin Press, 1974), 42.

59. Lacoue-Labarthe and Nancy, *The Literary Absolute*, 42.

60. Maurice Blanchot, "Athenaeum," in *The Infinite Conversation*, trans. Susan Hanson (Minneapolis, MN: University of Minnesota Press, 1993), 359.

61. *Ibid.*, 359.

62. Hegel, *Aesthetics: Lectures on Fine Art*, Volume 1, trans. T. M. Knox (Oxford: Clarendon Press, 1975), 64–69.

Reprint Permissions

We would like to thank the publishers indicated below for permission to reprint brief fragments from the following publications:

Giorgio Agamben, *The End of the Poem: Studies in Poetics*. Translated by Daniel Heller-Roazen (Palo Alto: Stanford University Press, 1999).

C.P. Cavafy, *Selected Poems*. Translated by Edmund Keeley & Philip Sherrard (Princeton, NJ: Princeton University Press, 1972).

Philippe Lacoue-Labarthe, *Poetry as Experience*. Translated by Andrea Tarnowski (Palo Alto: Stanford University Press, 1999).

Leo Strauss, *On Plato's Symposium*. Edited and with a Foreword by Seth Benardete (Chicago, Il: University of Chicago Press, 2001).

Index

Note: Page numbers followed by 'n' refer to notes

wit: material 111; and Romantic fragment 111–15
Wittgenstein, L. 11, 40–2; the example 92;
   Philosophical Investigations 77; on Shakespeare 83
word: elemental 45; written 55–6
words 86

writer: homelessness of 60
writing: concept 4, 51–60; indirect 55
written word 55–6

Xenophon 57